A Laboratory Manual of VETERINARY MICROBIOLOGY

A Laboratory Manual of VETERINARY MICROBIOLOGY

Part IV

Virology

B.S. Malik

Formerly : Professor and Head, Department of Bacteriology,
College of Veterinary Science and A.H., Mathura;
Professor and Head, Department of Microbiology, and
Dean, College and Faculty of Veterinary Science and A.H.,
J.N. Kashi Vishwa Vidyalaya, Jabalpur, India

CBS

CBS Publishers & Distributors Pvt. Ltd.

NEW DELHI • BANGALORE • PUNE • COCHIN • CHENNAI (INDIA)

By the same author :

MCQs and Short Answer Questions in Veterinary Bacteriology and Mycology

MCQs and Short Answer Questions in Veterinary Virology

A Laboratory Manual of Veterinary Microbiology (in four parts)

- Part I : General Bacteriology
- Part II : Immunology and Serology
- Part III : Pathogenic Bacteriology and Mycology
- Part IV : Virology

ISBN : 81-239-0495-9

First Edition : 1967
Second Edition : 1986
Reprint : 1988
Third Edition : 1992
Fourth Edition : 1996
Reprint : 1999, 2002, 2003, 2006, 2007, 2008, 2010

Published by Satish Kumar Jain and produced by V.K. Jain for
CBS Publishers & Distributors Pvt. Ltd.,
CBS Plaza, 4819/XI Prahlad Street, 24 Ansari Road, Daryaganj,
New Delhi - 110002, India. • Website: www.cbspd.com
e-mail: delhi@cbspd.com, cbspubs@vsnl.com, cbspubs@airtelmail.in
Ph.: 23289259, 23266861, 23266867 • Fax: 011-23243014

Branches:

- ***Bangalore:*** Seema House, 2975, 17th Cross, K.R. Road, Bansankari 2nd Stage, Bangalore - 560070 Ph.: 26771678/79 Fax: 080-26771680 • e-mail: bangalore@cbspd.com
- ***Pune:*** Shaan Brahmha Complex, 631/632, Basement, Appa Balwant Chowk, Budhwar Peth, Next to Ratan Talkies, Pune - 411002 Ph.: 020-24464057/58 • Fax: 020-24464059 e-mail: pune@cbspd.com
- ***Cochin:*** 36/14, Kalluvilakam, Lissie Hospital Road, Cochin - 682018, Kerala • e-mail: cochin@cbspd.com Ph.: 0484-4059061-65 • Fax: 0484-4059065
- ***Chennai:*** 20, West Park Road, Shenoy Nagar, Chennai - 600030 e-mail: chennai@cbspd.com Ph.: 044-26260666-26202620 Fax: 044-45530020

Printed at : J.S. Offset Printers, Delhi

Preface to the Fourth Edition

The first three editions of this manual have served their purpose to a great extent. The need for a laboratory manual is now felt all the more in view of the recommendations of the Veterinary Council of India (V.C.I.) to give more emphasis on practical teaching for B.V.Sc. & A.H. classes. The present edition of the manual has been divided into four separate parts, viz, Part I — General Bacteriology, Part II — Immunology and Serology, Part III — Pathogenic Bacteriology and Mycology, and Part IV — Virology. Laboratory exercises in virology have been added for the first time in the manual and presented as Part IV.

In the present edition, recent information has been incorporated as far as possible. Seventeen new exercises have been added in Part II and three additional exercises in Part III. The exercises on *Rickettsia* and *Chlamydia* have been added for the first time in Part III. The text portion of most of the exercises has been revised and enlarged.

It is hoped that this edition of the manual will fulfil the requirements of the course syllabus which is revised from time to time depending upon the new information and needs of the future graduates of veterinary science and animal husbandry.

Date : 15th June, 1995
Suryanagar, Ghaziabad, U.P.

B.S. MALIK

Acknowledgements

I am thankful to some of my colleagues and friends for their constant encouragement and constructive suggestions in the preparation and revision of the laboratory manual. The help from various textbooks, laboratory manuals and other sources is gratefully acknowledged.

I express my deep sense of gratitude to Mr. Satish Kumar Jain and Mr. Vinod Kumar Jain for their interest, cooperation and help in the publication of the manual within a short period. I also appreciate and admire the excellent technical and expert knowledge of Mr. Dharmvir who has taken pains and meticulous care in designing and presenting the book in the present form.

B.S. MALIK

Preface to the First Edition

Many of us who are engaged in teaching of Bacteriology in this country, feel that more stress should be laid on the bacteriological techniques and practical aspect of teaching. The author also shared this opinion and felt the need of a suitable laboratory guide which is hardly available in this country for successful implementation of such a programme.

For the last about two years the teaching programme in the Department of Bacteriology at U.P. College of Veterinary Science and Animal Husbandry, Mathura has been followed on the lines indicated in the manual. Students, laboratory staff and the teachers have very much liked this teaching approach. This has encouraged the author to introduce the "Laboratory Manual for Bacteriology and Immunology" for a systematic and methodical training in the subject. This is likely to fulfil the long felt demand of such a book in this country. By the availability of such a laboratory manual, the students will have an opportunity to read the exercise before coming to the class. Laboratory staff can arrange things and make preparations well in time according to the requirements of the class. The teachers have an advantage to follow a preplanned schedule of laboratory exercises which are laid down in the manual in a proper sequence.

The manual has been divided into four parts. Part I deals with the exercises on General Bacteriology, Part II on Immunology and Serology, Part III on Pathogenic Bacteriology and Part IV on Mycology. Part I gives the students a basic approach to the subject and acquaints them with various techniques and fundamental knowledge of Bacteriology. This prepares them for the study of pathogenic bacteria and fungi described in Part III and Part IV of the manual. Medical and Veterinary students should also be familiar with the principles of Immunity and hence various techniques in serological procedures have also been described in Part II of the manual.

Each exercise is introduced with the text material which will orient the students with the subject. Brief stepwise instructions have been given to perform the exercises. Wherever required, tables, blank spaces or charts have been provided to note down the results and observations. The questions after the exercises will stimulate the students to seek more informations on the subject by consulting extra literature a list of which is given in the end of the manual. The answers of the questions are intended to be written on a supplementary answer book and shown to the teachers.

Formulae and details of the preparation of certain reagents, etc., are given in the appendix. Instructions for the post-mortem examination of laboratory animals and for the collection, preservation and the despatch of the bacteriological material for laboratory examination are also provided in the appendix.

By using this book as a guide, if the students get a clear understanding and a systematic and methodical approach to the subject, the purpose of writing this manual is accomplished. The author earnestly hopes that the book will meet the long felt demand of such a manual in this country. The author will be grateful to those who would point out the faults and omissions, if any, which might have been left in this edition.

Contents

LIST OF EQUIPMENTS FOR VIROLOGICAL WORK

1. Inoculation booth with laminar flow
2. Microscopes (including inverted microscope)
3. Autoclave
4. Hot air oven
5. Electric sterilizer
6. Refrigerator
7. Deep freezer
8. Incubators (including B.O.D. and egg incubators)
9. Water bath
10. Centrifuges (including refrigerated and ultracentrifuges)
11. Dental drill
12. Egg candler
13. Freeze dryer
14. Various grades of filters
15. Vacuum and pressure pump
16. Glass distillation apparatus
17. Scissors, forceps, post-mortem set, etc.
18. Neutral glass flasks, test tubes, petridishes, pipettes and syringes
19. Chemicals, tissue culture and other media, reagents, normal saline solution, distilled water, stains, disinfecting solution, etc.

MATERIALS REQUIRED FOR GENERAL USE

For individual student to be provided by the student

	Item	Quantity
1.	Laboratory coat	2
2.	Drawing pencil	1
3.	Scale	1
4.	Match box	1
5.	Muslin cloth	½ yard
6.	Scissors	1
7.	Forceps	1

Materials to be supplied by the department

	Item	Quantity
8.	Wax glass marking pencil	½
9.	Cheese cloth for mopping and cleaning the table	1 yard
10.	Blotting paper sheet	½
11.	Microscope slides (3″ × 1″)	10
12.	Micro-cover slips	4
13.	Hanging drop slides	2
14.	Inoculation loop	1
15.	Bunsen burner	1
16.	Microscope (between two students)	1
17.	Microscope lamp (between two students)	1
18.	Immersion oil bottle (between two students)	1

Materials for general class use

Stains
Disinfecting solution
Sterilized pipettes
Sterilized flasks
Sterilized normal saline
Water path
Colony counter
Rubber bulbs and Pasteur pipettes
Incubator
Wash bottles
Biochemical and other reagents
Sterilized petri dishes
Sterilized cotton wool
Sterilized distilled water
Thermometers
Electric sterilizer
Tissue paper books
Autoclave and hot air oven

Part IV

Virology

Nature of Viruses

Viruses are submicroscopic. They contain either DNA or RNA as their genome which is enclosed in a protein coat known as capsid. A complete or mature virus is known as virion. The capsid is composed of identical sub-units or structural units called capsomeres. The symmetry of capsid is either cubical or helical types except in case of pox viruses where it is complex type. The capsid together with enclosed nucleic acid is known as nucleocapsid.

Viruses multiply only in living cells. Viruses infect human beings, animals, plants and insects. Some of them cause severe diseases in their hosts. The viruses infecting bacteria are known as bacteriophages. The nucleic acids of the viruses contain necessary information and direct the infected cells of the host to synthesize virus specific macromolecules for their replication.

The size of the viruses varies from 20 to 350 nm. The viruses are classified on the basis of DNA or RNA, size, whether enveloped or not, number of capsomeres in the capsid, presence or absence of transcriptase and the nature of genome which includes whether the nucleic acid is single or double stranded, whether the genome is segmented or nonsegmented, whether strands are (+) or (–), molecular weight and whether replication takes place in host cell nucleus or cytoplasm.

Important characteristics of DNA and RNA virus families are shown in Table 1.

Table 1. Important characteristics of virus families

Family	Size (nm)	Envelope	Symmetry of capsid	No. of capsomeres	Transcriptase	Nature of genome
DNA viruses						
1. Papovaviridae	45 × 55	–	Icosahedral	72	–	DNA, C, NS, DS
2. Adenoviridae	70	–	Icosahedral	252	–	DNA, L, NS, DS
3. Herpesviridae	150-170	+	Icosahedral	162	–	DNA, L, NS, DS
4. Poxviridae	200 × 300	+	Complex	—	+	DNA, L, NS, DS
5. Parvoviridae	20	–	Icosahedral	32	–	DNA, L, NS, SS (–)
6. Iridoviridae	220	+	Icosahedral	1892	+	DNA, L, NA, DS
7. Hepadnaviridae	45	–	Icosahedral	?	+ (reverse)	DNA, C, NS, DS
RNA viruses						
8. Picornaviridae	25	–	Icosahedral	60	–	RNA, L, NS, SS (+)
9. Coronaviridae	100	+	Helical	—	–	RNA, L, NS, SS (+)
10. Caliciviridae	35	–	Icosahedral	32	–	RNA, L, NS, SS (+)
11. Togaviridae	65	+	Icosahedral	?	–	RNA, L, NS, SS (+)
12. Flaviviridae	45	+	Icosahedral	?	–	RNA, L, NS, SS (+)
13. Orthomyxoviridae	100	+	Helical	—	+	RNA, L, S-8, SS (–)
14. Paramyxoviridae	180	+	Helical	—	+	RNA, L, NS, SS (–)
15. Rhabdoviridae	180 × 70	+	Helical	—	+	RNA, L, NS, SS (–)
16. Arenaviridae	120	+	Helical	—	+	RNA, L, S-2, SS (–)
17. Bunyaviridae	110	+	Helical	—	+	RNA, L, S-3, SS (–)
18. Reoviridae	60-80	–	Icosahedral	32, 92	+	RNA, L, S10-12, DS
19. Retroviridae	100	+	Icosahedral	?	+ (reverse)	RNA, L, NS, SS (+)
20. Birnaviridae	55-63	–	Icosahedral	92	+	RNA, L, S-2, DS

C = circular; L = linear; S = segmented; NS = nonsegmented; DS = double stranded; SS = single stranded; (+) = plus strand; (–) = minus strand.

EXERCISE 1

COLLECTION AND PRESERVATION OF VIRAL SPECIMENS

Specimens from virus infected animals should be collected early in the course of the disease when maximum amount of virus is expected to be present before any treatment and production of antibodies in the system. Blood, faeces, sputum, nasal discharge, skin lesions etc. can be collected from clinical cases. Depending upon the predilection of the virus infecting certain tissues, they can be collected at the time of post-mortem. As an example, skin lesions can be collected from animals suffering from pox diseases; trachea, bronchi and lungs from cases suffering from respiratory infections; brain and spinal cord from cases suffering from neurotropic viruses affecting central nervous system. Other organs like spleen, liver, lungs, kidneys, lymph glands etc. can be collected from generalized infections affecting most of the organs. Sera for antibody testing should be collected from recovered animals after 1 week of recovery.

After collection of the specimens, they should be preserved by freezing or freeze drying till they are used for inoculation in animals, embryonated eggs or cell cultures. The specimens can be transported to the laboratory in thermos flask containing dry ice. If the specimen is not used immediately, it should be preserved at –45°C or lower temperature in deep freezer. The temperature of storage cabinet with dry ice is about –70°C. The specimens should be collected in good quality screw-cap vials so that they can withstand repeated freezing and thawing. Specimens for long preservation (and for vaccine preparations) can be freeze dried under vacuum. The freeze dried vials (sealed) can be stored in ordinary refrigerator at 4°C.

Materials

Fowls infected with Ranikhet (Newcastle) disease, fowl pox, infectious laryngotracheitis, infectious bronchitis, infectious bursal disease and avian encephalomyelitis; instruments for post-mortem examination, screw-cap vials for specimen collection, 2% citrated saline, thioglycollate broth tubes, blood agar plates, deep freezer maintaining temperature at –45°C or lower.

Procedure

1. Collect blood from all the chickens from heart or wing vein. Place one portion of the

blood in 2% citrated saline in proportion of 9 parts of blood and 1 part of citrated saline for collection of plasma. The other portion of the blood will be used for collection of serum.

2. Centrifuge the citrated blood at 1000 RPM for 10 minutes and transfer the plasma (supernatant) to a screw-cap vial. Place the other portion of the blood (clotted) in a slanting position in the refrigerator and next day separate serum in a screw-cap vial.
3. Kill the infected birds, perform post-mortem examination, collect following specimens in screw-cap vials : Newcastle disease—lung, spleen and kidney; fowl pox—skin, feather follicles, and comb lesions; infectious laryngotracheitis—trachea and lung; infectious bronchitis—trachea and lung; infectious bursal disease—bursa of Fabricius; avian encephalomyelitis—brain.
4. Inoculate thioglycollate broth and blood agar plates with each sample for bacteriological sterility test.
5. Preserve the specimens including plasma and serum in a deep freezer at –45°C or lower temperature till they are needed for inoculation. All samples should be labelled properly with details.

Results

Record the following observations :

Disease	Pathological changes on post-mortem	Bacterial growth on media	
		Thioglycollate broth (+ or –)	Blood agar (+ or –)
Ranikhet disease			
Fowl pox			
Infectious laryngotracheitis			
Infectious bronchitis			
Infectious bursal disease			
Avian encephalomyelitis			

QUESTIONS

1. If ice or deep freezer or even refrigerator facilities are not available, what other method(s) can be employed to preserve viral specimens temporarily?

2. Why cotton wool stoppered test tubes are not used to preserve viral specimens in dry ice cabinet?
3. What specimens will be collected from following animals?
   (a) Cattle infected with foot and mouth disease.
   (b) Cattle infected with rinderpest.
   (c) Sheep infected with sheep pox.
   (d) Sheep infected with blue tongue disease.
   (e) Swine infected with hog cholera.
   (f) Dog infected with rabies.
   (g) Dog infected with distemper.
   (h) Equine infected with equine influenza.

EXERCISE 2

PREPARATION OF VIRUS SPECIMENS FOR INOCULATION

Tissues for virus isolation are to be grounded in a mortar and pestle with the help of an abrasive like powdered glass, sand or alundum. (Good quality hard sand should be properly washed in distilled water, treated with hydrochloric acid, washed thoroughly, dried and sterilized before use.) The diluent should be nutrient broth, tryptose phosphate broth or phosphate buffered saline. Normally the concentration of the tissue in the inoculum is about 10-20%. While grinding the tissues, the temperature should be kept as low as possible. When the tissue is likely to be contaminated, the inoculum should be treated with antibiotics.

Materials

Frozen specimens from Exercise No. 1, mortars and pestles, sterile sand, broth, syringes and needles.

Procedure

1. Take out the frozen specimens from deep freezer and thaw them at room temperature. Transfer the specimen to a mortar, cut it into small pieces, add small quantity of sterile sand and broth and grind into a fine paste, add more broth and grind again. The amount of diluent should be added to make it about 10-20%. The suspension should then be transferred to the original screw-cap tube with the help of a pipette. Add penicillin and streptomycin at the rate of 10,000 units and 10 mg per ml respectively and incubate at room temperature for 20 minutes. The suspension is then centrifuged at 2500 RPM for 20 minutes to sediment the coarse particles. The supernatant fluid is removed in another tube and used as inoculum in the suitable host system.
2. The frozen plasma and serum are removed from deep freezer and thawed. If they are found contaminated on sterility test, they should also be treated with penicillin and streptomycin before use as inoculum in suitable host.

QUESTIONS

1. Briefly describe the method of freezing and drying.
2. What is the role of liquid nitrogen in preservation of tissues for virus isolation.
3. Why broth or phosphate buffer saline and not normal saline solution are recommended as diluent for preparing virus inoculum?

Methods to Study Physical Properties of Viruses

Equipments used for centrifugation, electrophoresis, filtration and electron microscopy are very useful tools to study physical properties of the viruses. Ultracentrifugation is used to determine the size, shape and density of the viruses, ultrafiltration to determine the size, shape and possibly electrical charge of the virus, electrophoresis for surface potential and possibly size of the viruses and other biological substances and electron microscopy is used to determine the size, shape and structural arrangement of viruses or their subunits and also for counting virus particles. Ultra-thin sections and intracellular aspect of viral multiplication can also be studied by electron microscopy.

Centrifugation

The ordinary laboratory centrifuges have a low centrifugal force and are used to separate tissue elements from viruses. Sedimentation of virus particles requires high centrifugal force for which ultracentrifuge is required. Examples of ultracentrifuges are :

1. **Preparative ultracentrifuge :** Example : Model L, Spinco Division, Beckman Instruments, Inc., Palo Alto, California, USA.
2. **Analytical ultracentrifuge :** Example : Model E, Spinco Division, Beckman Instruments, Inc., Palo Alto, California.

   Both the above models are extremely advanced and work under refrigeration system. The RPMs of model L are from 0 to 50,000 and that of E model from 0 to 60,000.
3. **Sharples Corporation Super-centrifuge :** This is used for continuous flow of liquid due to centrifugal force in a rotating cylinder with an inlet at the bottom and outlet discharge on the top.

Electrophoresis

This is a method for studying migration of charged particles in solution in an electrical field. This technique is mostly used to study serum, plasma and to some extent viruses. Several companies are marketing many models of electrophoresis instruments. The students may be aware of the working of this instrument in the Department of Biochemistry and in the Serology course while working for immuno-electrophoresis technique.

Electron microscopy

This is a counterpart of light microscope. It utilizes high potential in the production of an electronic beam in a vacuum chamber with electro-magnetic lenses instead of light rays and glass lenses used in light microscope. The theoretical lower limit of resolution with electron microscope is a small fraction of an angstrom unit but in practice the maximum limit of resolution is about 10 to 20 angstrom (1 to 2 mμ). The electron image is a shadow of the object. Viruses have low density. If the density of the object is increased, electron image will be sharper and well-defined. The metal shadow casting greatly enhances the quality of electron micrographs. Shadow casting is done with a thin film of gold, chromium or some other metal which is evaporated at an angle on the object which is mounted on a supporting collodion film.

The negative staining technique with a heavy metal salt like phosphotungstic acid or some other compound permits examination of detailed structures of viruses. The nucleic acid content of viruses can be determined by positive staining with uranyl acetate as DNA viruses stain with this compound and not RNA viruses.

As far as possible the instructor should explain different models and working of these equipments. These instruments are specialized equipments and are handled by trained technicians. The working of such instruments should be demonstrated to the students.

Filtration

Filters are used to separate viruses from gross particles and bacteria. Different grades of filters are used to find out the size of viruses. The techniques of filtration are demonstrated in Exercise 3.

EXERCISE 3

FILTERS AND TECHNIQUES OF FILTRATION

Filters are used for sterilization of some thermostable materials like blood sera, sugar media etc. The main purposes of the use of filters in virology laboratory are :

1. To clarify media by removing gross particles.
2. To remove bacteria from viruses.
3. To selectively separate large sized bacteria from smaller bacteria, larger viruses from smaller viruses and to roughly estimate the size of viruses.

The disadvantages in the use of filters are, difficulty in their cleaning and sterilization and also on account of absorption of viruses during filtration.

For other details of filters and filtration the students can refer to Exercise No. 6 of Laboratory Manual of Veterinary Microbiology, Part I, General Bacteriology.

Materials

Different types of filters and other equipments used in filtration.

Procedure

1. Demonstration of the construction of filters.
2. Demonstration of assembling and sterilization of filters.
3. Demonstration of techniques of filtration by different filters.

QUESTIONS

1. Name the factors involved in the process of filtration.
2. How would you determine the size of viruses by filtration?
3. What are the differences between light microscope and electron microscope?
4. Why metal shadow casting technique is necessary for taking electron micrographs of viruses by electron microscope.

Cultivation of Viruses

Viruses can be cultivated only in living cells. For their cultivation, living cells are available in :

A. Natural hosts and laboratory animals
B. Embryonated eggs
C. Cell culture system

A. Cultivation of viruses in natural hosts and laboratory animals

In most cases attempts are made to cultivate the viruses in embryonated eggs or cell cultures which are more convenient and economical than animals. However to find out the course of the disease, the clinical symptoms, pathogenicity and post-mortem lesions, the viruses have to be inoculated in the natural hosts and laboratory animals. Cultivation of viruses in laboratory animals are preferred rather than in the natural hosts. There are some viruses which can be cultivated only in natural hosts. When viruses are grown in animals, the animals should be healthy, disease-free and free from antibodies.

In animals some viruses have preference to grow in certain tissues like skin, respiratory system, nervous system etc., while others can grow in all organs and tissues. The route of inoculation has to be selected according to the possible tissue predilection of the viruses. Different routes of inoculation may be intramuscular (I/M), subcutaneous (S/C), intravenous (I/V), intraperitoneal (I/P), intranasal (I/N), and intracerebral (I/C). Laboratory animals for virological studies are mice, guinea pigs, rabbits, monkeys, hamsters and chickens. The students are advised to refer to Exercises 1, 2 and 3 of A Laboratory Manual of Veterinary Microbiology, Part II, Immunology & Serology by the author for care and handling, methods of injections and bleeding the laboratory animals.

EXERCISE 4

CULTIVATION OF FOWL POX VIRUS IN CHICKENS

Materials

Fowl pox virus-infected skin from Exercise 1, 4-months old healthy susceptible chickens, and equipments for inoculation.

Procedure

1. Take out the fowl pox infected skin from deep freezer and thaw it at room temperature.
2. Prepare the specimen for inoculation as described in Exercise 2.
3. After centrifuging the suspension at 2500 RPM for 20 minutes, transfer 1 ml supernatant fluid in another tube. Return the remaining infected skin/suspension in the deep freezer for future use.
4. Inoculate one chicken by feather follicle method : Remove few feathers from one side of the leg and swab the defeathered follicles with a stiff-bristled brush dipped in fowl pox fluid.
5. Inoculate other chicken with fowl pox fluid by stick method. For this, dip the point of inoculation needle in the fowl pox fluid and pierce the skin of the chicken on lateral surface of the leg.
6. Return the chickens in individual cages and examine the site of inoculation daily up to 12-15 days. Takes will indicate swollen follicles and scab formation on the skin about 8th to 12th days after inoculation.
7. Specimens may be collected on 6th to 7th day of inoculation from infected skin.

Results

Note down the type of skin lesions and other clinical symptoms of the chickens and record the observations in the table on the next page.

QUESTIONS

1. What is the size, type of symmetry of the capsid, and nature of genome of fowl pox virus?

Chicken No.	Clinical symptoms and lesions on post-inoculation days
1 (Inoculated by feather follicle method)	
2 (Inoculated by stick method)	

2. Name antigenic relationship, if any, among the fowl pox, canary pox and pigeon pox viruses.
3. Briefly describe the following :
   (a) Type of fowl pox vaccine(s) used in India
   (b) Whether the virus is cultivated in fowls, eggs or cell cultures
   (c) Whether the vaccine is killed or attenuated
   (d) The dose, route and age of vaccination
   (e) Duration of immunity.
4. Describe the symptoms and lesions of different forms of fowl pox.

EXERCISE 5

CULTIVATION OF RANIKHET DISEASE VIRUS IN CHICKENS

Materials

Lung and spleen from Ranikhet disease infected chickens (from Exercise 1), 4-6 weeks old disease-free chickens 2, equipments for inoculation and for post-mortem.

Procedure

1. Take out from deep freezer lung and spleen tissues from Ranikhet disease infected chicken and prepare inoculum as described in Exercise 2.
2. Inoculate 4-6 weeks old chickens with 0.4 ml inoculum. Half of the dose should be given I/M and the other half by I/N route. Return the chickens to the cage.
3. Examine the chickens for clinical symptoms every day. On 3rd or 4th day of inoculation, the birds may show respiratory distress, nervous symptoms and other clinical symptoms.
4. When clinical symptoms are evident, kill the birds with cervical dislocation and perform post-mortem examination. Examine lesions in trachea, lungs and other internal organs.
5. Collect trachea, lungs, spleen and brain in a screw-cap tube and store in the deep freezer.

Results

Note down the clinical symptoms and post-mortem lesions in the following table.

Chicken No.	Clinical symptoms and lesions on post-mortem examination
1	
2	

QUESTIONS

1. Based on virulence, classify Ranikhet disease virus strains. Name virus strains falling within each of these categories.
2. Name different Ranikhet disease vaccines used in India, their doses, route of vaccination and age of chicks/chickens when vaccinated.
3. How is R_2B Ranikhet disease vaccine prepared?
4. Name major characteristics of Ranikhet disease virus and antigenic relationship with other animal viruses.
5. What are the criteria to determine the virulence of Ranikhet disease virus?
6. Give a schedule of Ranikhet disease vaccination.

EXERCISE 6

CULTIVATION OF FOOT AND MOUTH DISEASE VIRUS IN GUINEA PIG FOOT PAD

Materials

Foot and mouth disease virus (type O) preferably in the form of lymph from cattle tongue vesicles, about 2 months old guinea pigs 2, equipments for inoculation.

Procedure

1. Remove the frozen FMD lymph (or other material) from deep freezer and prepare inoculum as described in Exercise 2.
2. Inoculate 2 guinea pigs on foot pad as follows :
   (a) Clean one hind foot pad of each guinea pig with 70% alcohol and dry.
   (b) Mark one longitudinal line on the sterilized foot pad of each guinea pig and intradermally inoculate 0.1 ml with 25 gauge ½ inch needle at five equidistant spots on the marked line on foot pads.
3. The guinea pigs are returned to individual cages with good bedding and observed daily for clinical symptoms and local lesions on the foot pads.
4. On 4th or 5th day when foot pad lesions are fully developed, the skin from inoculated foot pads is removed and frozen in a screw-cap tube in a deep freezer.

Results

Note down the clinical symptoms, if any, and the lesions on the foot pad and record in the following table.

Guinea pig No.	Clinical symptoms and lesions on foot pad on post-inoculation days				
	1	2	3	4	5
1					
2					

QUESTIONS

1. Name the family and genus of the FMD virus.
2. Name various types and number of subtypes of FMD virus.
3. Briefly describe the properties of FMD virus and name animal species which are infected with FMD virus.
4. Name the types of FMD vaccines used in India, the centres of vaccine production, dose and route of vaccination in different animals and the source (animal, eggs or cell cultures) of vaccine production.
5. FMD virus can be cultivated in suckling mice. Discuss briefly.
6. What are the serological tests used for typing various FMD virus strains?
7. Describe the clinical symptoms and lesions of FMD in :
   (a) cattle and buffaloes
   (b) pigs
   (c) sheep and goats.
8. How FMD virus persists among various livestock from season to season?

B. Cultivation of Viruses in Embryonating Chicken Eggs

Like animals, embryonated chicken eggs also possess highly specialized tissues and organs and are frequently utilized to grow various viruses particularly those infecting chickens and other birds. The usual routes of inoculation in chicken embryos are yolk sac method, chorioallantoic membrane (CAM) method, allantoic cavity and amniotic cavity routes. Intravenous and intracerebral routes are used in rare cases. Routes of inoculation in chicken embryos depend upon the viruses to be cultivated.

In the next few exercises the students will learn the techniques of inoculation in embryonated chicken eggs and harvesting the material after virus multiplication. For doing so they will use normal saline solution for learning the techniques before using virus inoculum in subsequent exercises. Cultivation of viruses in embryonating eggs is a convenient and economical method. The eggs should be used from disease-free stock. Eggs from vaccinated flock may carry antibodies in the yolk which may interfere in the growth of specific viruses. Some viruses may also pass through the eggs from infected birds to the chicks.

Some factors which affect the multiplication of the viruses in chicken egg are : Age of embryo, route of inoculation, concentration and volume of inoculum, temperature of incubation, and time of incubation after inoculation. Preliminary incubation temperature may be 38°C and 37°C after inoculation.

Embryonating eggs may be inoculated by several routes. Selection of the route depends upon the virus and its affinity to grow in certain tissue(s). The routes of inoculation are :

1. Yolk sac inoculation : Six to seven days incubated eggs are used for yolk sac inoculation. The volume of inoculum is 0.2-1.0 ml.
2. Chorioallantoic membrane route (CAM route) : Inoculation is made in 10-12 days old embryos. The quantity is 0.1-0.5 ml.
3. Allantoic cavity route : Inoculation is made in 9-12 days old embryos, the volume being 0.1-0.2 ml.
4. Amniotic cavity route : The age of the embryos varies from 7-15 days and the size of the inoculum is 0.1-0.2 ml.

The other routes of inoculation like intravenous and intracerebral are rarely used. The viruses of Ranikhet disease, infectious bronchitis, influenza and encephalitis are inoculated by allantoic route; fowl pox, infectious laryngotracheitis, Marek's disease and infectious bursal disease viruses by chorioallantoic membrane route and blue tongue and African swine fever viruses by yolk sac method. For primary isolation of influenza virus, amniotic cavity route is preferred.

After virus inoculation, the embryonated eggs are incubated, and examined daily by candling method. If embryos die within 24 hours, the death is considered non-specific (except arbo viruses) and such eggs are removed from the incubator and discarded. Some viruses, e.g., Ranikhet disease virus kill the embryos within 2-3 days. In other cases the eggs are allowed to incubate up to 5-6 days. The eggs are daily turned upside down. On primary isolation, some viruses may not kill the embryos or produce various pathological changes in first one or two inoculations.

To confirm whether some virus is responsible for the infection, repeated serial blind passages are given in the eggs before discarding them as negative. After few passages, the virus may start killing the embryos or produce other changes. These pathological changes may be :

(a) Haemorrhages of subcutaneous tissues.
(b) Curling and dwarfing of embryos.
(c) Thickening of chorioallantoic membrane.
(d) Pock lesions on chorioallantoic membrane.
(e) Decrease in the amount of amniotic fluid.
(f) Development of inclusion bodies in the cytoplasm or nucleus of infected cells.
(g) Improper development of feathers.

Immediately after the death of the embryos, or after termination of incubation period, the eggs should be removed from the incubator and chilled for several hours before collection of embryos or other materials.

The students should be acquainted with the developmental stages of embryonated chicken eggs and demonstrated various routes of inoculation as indicated in Fig. 1.

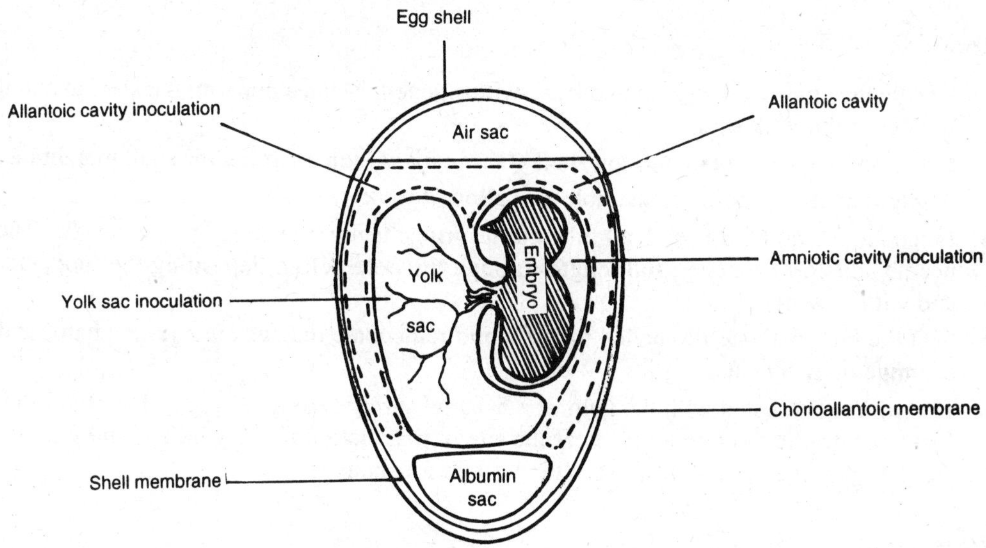

Fig. 1. Routes of inoculation in embryonated chicken eggs.

EXERCISE 7

INOCULATION OF EMBRYONATED CHICKEN EGGS WITH NORMAL SALINE SOLUTION (NSS) BY YOLK SAC METHOD

Materials

Seven days incubated embryonating chicken eggs, normal saline solution, egg drill machine, egg candler, syringes and needles, forceps, scissors, petridish, tincture of iodine, melted paraffin.

Method

1. Candle the eggs and locate the yolk sac with a pencil. Make a mark on the shell at about middle of the yolk sac.
2. Drill a small hole through the egg shell at the mark without piercing the shell membrane.
3. Apply tincture of iodine to the hole and allow it to dry.
4. Inoculate 0.5 ml NSS with 1 ml tuberculin syringe using 27 gauge ½ inch needle. The needle should be inserted full length through the hole before depositing the inoculum and withdrawing.
5. Seal the hole with sterile melted paraffin and reincubate the eggs in egg incubator and examine daily by candling for 3-4 days.
6. The yolk is harvested with the help of a 5-10 ml syringe using 20 gauge 1 inch needle. Insert the needle through a hole near the site of inoculation in the yolk sac and aspirate the yolk into the syringe and expel the yolk in a container.

Results

Record your observations regarding the death of the embryos and other pathological lesions, if any.

QUESTIONS

1. Name animal and poultry viruses which are normally inoculated by yolk sac method in embryonated chicken eggs.

EXERCISE 8

INOCULATION OF EMBRYONATED CHICKEN EGGS WITH NSS BY CHORIOALLANTOIC MEMBRANE (CAM) ROUTE

Materials

Ten to twelve days old embryonated chicken eggs, egg incubator, drill machine, egg candler, NSS, syringes and needles, forceps, scissors, petridish, tincture of iodine, melted paraffin.

Procedure

1. Candle the eggs and mark the position of embryos.
2. Keep the long axis of the egg in horizontal position with embryo uppermost, mark an equilateral triangle with each side about 1 cm.
3. With carborundum disk, cut the egg shell at the marks of the triangle without piercing through the shell membrane. Also make a pointed cut through the shell over the air sac.
4. Apply disinfectant on the cut areas of the shell and allow to dry.
5. Remove the shell over the triangle with the help of a needle or forceps to expose intact shell membrane.
6. With a needle, pierce the shell membrane over the air sac and on the side in the triangular area without piercing the chorioallantoic membrane.
7. Create a slight vacuum with a small rubber bulb at the hole over the air sac by sucking the air through the bulb. Air will pass through the opening in the shell membrane on the side of the egg allowing the CAM to drop from the shell membrane underneath the triangular area. The air sac area will be occupied by the embryo, membranes and fluids and an artificial air cell will be created on the side of the egg.
8. Use 1 ml tuberculin syringe with 27 gauge ½ inch needle and deposit 0.2 ml inoculum through the shell membrane over artificial air cell on CAM. Withdraw the needle.
9. Close the triangular opening in the shell with a suitable sized adhesive tape. Also seal the hole over the normal air sac space with melted paraffin or adhesive tape.
10. Incubate the eggs in egg incubator and examine and turn them daily for 3-4 days.
11. To collect the CAM, apply disinfectant on the shell area over artificial air cell. Remove the shell and shell membrane over artificial air cell with forceps to expose CAM. Cut

the artificial air cell portion of CAM using scissors, clean the membrane with NSS in a petridish and place the membrane in a container.

Results

Record observations regarding death of embryos and pathological lesions, if any.

QUESTIONS

1. Name the viruses which can be grown in embryonated chicken eggs by CAM route. Also name viruses which produce pock lesions on CAM.
2. Name poultry viral diseases which produce intracytoplasmic and intranuclear inclusion bodies in CAM cells.

EXERCISE 9

INOCULATION OF EMBRYONATED CHICKEN EGGS WITH NSS BY ALLANTOIC CAVITY ROUTE

Materials

Embryonated chicken eggs incubated for 10 days, egg incubator, drill machine, egg candler, NSS, syringes and needles, forceps, scissors, petridish, tincture of iodine and melted paraffin.

Procedure

1. While candling the eggs, mark an area of CAM away from the embryo and amniotic cavity. The area should be free from large blood vessels and about 3-4 mm below the base of the air sac.
2. Make another mark on the upper end of the air sac of the eggs.
3. Drill a hole at each of the two marks through the shell. Do not pierce the shell membrane. Disinfect the shell on the drilled holes.
4. With sterile precautions, make a small puncture in the shell membrane in the hole over the air sac.
5. Inoculate 0.2 ml NSS through the hole in the side of the egg to a depth of about ¼ inch. Use 1 ml tuberculin syringe with 27 gauge ½ inch needle.
6. Seal the two holes with melted paraffin and incubate the eggs for 4-5 days.
7. For collection of allantoic fluid, apply disinfectant to the shell over air sac. Break the shell over air sac with forceps and remove the shell to a distance of about 8-10 mm from the top of the air sac.
8. With the help of a 10 ml syringe and 22 gauge 1 inch needle, collect about 5 ml allantoic fluid from the cavity through air sac opening and expel the fluid in a container.

Results

Record observations including death of embryos and other pathological lesion, if any.

QUESTIONS

1. Name the viruses which can be grown in embryonated chicken eggs via allantoic route.

EXERCISE 10

INOCULATION OF EMBRYONATED CHICKEN EGGS WITH NSS VIA AMNIOTIC CAVITY ROUTE

Materials

Embryonated chicken eggs 7-15 days preincubated, egg incubator, drill machine, egg candler, NSS, syringes and needles, forceps, scissors, petridish, tincture of iodine and melted paraffin.

Procedure

1. Candle the eggs and make a mark with pencil on the shell below the base of the air sac to locate the embryo in each egg.
2. Draw a circle about 5 mm above the base of the air sac.
3. With drill, cut the egg shell at the circle mark without piercing the shell membrane.
4. Apply disinfectant to the cut mark on the circle.
5. Remove the shell over air sac with forceps and expose the shell membrane.
6. Apply few drops of sterile saline solution or light mineral oil to the shell membrane over the embryo to make the membrane transparent.
7. Using 1 ml tuberculin syringe fitted with 27 gauge 1 inch needle, deposit 0.2 ml inoculum by inserting the needle into amniotic cavity.
8. Close the opening over the air sac with sterile thick white paper disk sealing it with melted paraffin. Incubate the eggs.
9. For harvesting the amniotic fluid, remove the paper disk from the air sac of the eggs.
10. First remove allantoic fluid as described in case of allantoic cavity route (Exercise 9). Remove shell membrane and CAM from the base of air sac. This will give a better view of the amnion. With another syringe and needle, aspirate amniotic fluid from amniotic cavity. Expel the fluid in a container.

Results

Record the observations including the death of the embryos, if any.

QUESTIONS

1. Name the viruses which are cultivated in embryonated chicken eggs by amniotic cavity route.

EXERCISE 11

CULTIVATION OF INFECTIOUS BRONCHITIS (IB) VIRUS IN EMBRYONATED CHICKEN EGGS BY ALLANTOIC CAVITY ROUTE

Materials

Lungs and trachea from infectious bronchitis infected chicken (from Exercise 1), 10 days old chicken embryos 5, egg incubator, drill machine, egg candler, syringes and needles, forceps, scissors, petridish, tincture of iodine, melted paraffin, phosphate buffer saline, penicillin and streptomycin.

Procedure

1. Remove the lung and tracheal tissues of IB infected chicken from deep freezer and thaw at room temperature.
2. Triturate the tissues in mortar and pestle with the help of abrasive, prepare 10% suspension and centrifuge at 2500 RPM for 20 minutes.
3. Remove the supernatant and treat it with penicillin and streptomycin at room temperature for 20 minutes. Fill 0.6 ml in 1 ml syringe and use for egg inoculation. Also test the suspension for sterility by inoculation on blood agar plates and thioglycollate broth.
4. Inoculate 5 eggs with 0.1 ml fluid per egg by allantoic cavity route, and incubate at 37°C.
5. Candle the eggs daily and frequently turn the eggs upside down. Any death within 24 hours of inoculation is considered non-specific and such eggs are discarded.
6. Eggs dying after 3rd day are removed from incubator and their allantoic fluid is preserved in deep freezer for future use.
7. On 7th day remove all the remaining eggs and examine the embryos for pathological lesions, and record the observations in the following table.

Results

Note down the embryo mortality, if any, and record pathological lesions in embryos in the table on the next page.

Embryo No.	Day of mortality	Pathological lesions
1		
2		
3		
4		
5		

QUESTIONS

1. Describe the pathological changes in the chicken embryos due to infectious bronchitis virus.
2. Differentiate the viruses of infectious bronchitis, infectious laryngotracheitis, Ranikhet disease and fowl pox under laboratory conditions.
3. Name different strains of infectious bronchitis virus including those used for vaccine production.

EXERCISE 12

CULTIVATION OF RANIKHET DISEASE (R.D.) VIRUS IN EMBRYONATED CHICKEN EGGS BY ALLANTOIC CAVITY ROUTE

Materials

Ranikhet disease infected chicken lung, kidney and spleen tissues (from Exercise 1), 10 days old embryonated chicken eggs 5, egg incubator, drill machine, egg candler, syringes and needles, forceps, scissors, petridish, tincture of iodine, melted paraffin, phosphate buffer saline, penicillin and streptomycin.

Procedure

1. Take out the R.D. infected tissues from deep freezer and thaw at room temperature.
2. Triturate the tissues in mortar and pestle, prepare 10% suspension and centrifuge at 2500 RPM for 20 minutes. Remove supernatant in a test tube and add penicillin and streptomycin at the rate of 10,000 units and 10 mg per ml respectively and allow to act for 20 minutes at room temperature.
3. Inoculate 5 eggs by allantoic cavity route using 0.1 ml inoculum per egg and incubate them in egg incubator. The sterility of the fluid should be tested on blood agar plate and in thioglycollate medium.
4. Examine the eggs daily and collect dead eggs at 48-72 hours. Keep the eggs in refrigerator for few hours and collect allantoic fluid and preserve in deep freezer.
5. Examine the embryos for pathological lesions.

Results

Note down the embryo mortality, their pathological changes and other abnormality in the table on the next page.

QUESTIONS

1. Briefly describe pathogenicity of R.D. virus in young and adult birds.
2. Name Ranikhet disease vaccines and merits and demerits of each.

Embryo No.	Day of death	Pathological changes
1		
2		
3		
4		
5		

EXERCISE 13

CULTIVATION OF INFECTIOUS LARYNGOTRACHEITIS (ILT) VIRUS IN EMBRYONATED CHICKEN EGGS BY CHORIOALLANTOIC MEMBRANE ROUTE

Materials

ILT infected chicken trachea and lung tissues (from Exercise 1), 10-12 days old embryonated chicken eggs 5, egg incubator, drill machine, egg candler, syringes and needles, forceps, scissors, petridish, tincture of iodine, melted paraffin, phosphate buffer saline, penicillin and streptomycin.

Procedure

1. Take out the lung and tracheal tissues from deep freezer and thaw at room temperature. Triturate the tissues in mortar and pestle and prepare 10% suspension.
2. Centrifuge the material at 2500 RPM for 20 minutes.
3. Remove the supernatant in a tube and treat with penicillin and streptomycin for 20 minutes at room temperature. Fill 1 ml in a syringe for egg inoculation and sterility test on blood agar plate and in thioglycollate medium.
4. Inoculate 5 eggs by CAM route, the amount of inoculum being 0.1 ml in each egg.
5. Incubate the eggs at 37°C in egg incubator for 4-5 days. Examine eggs daily and note down deaths, if any. Dead embryos should be removed and stored in refrigerator.
6. Remove all the remaining eggs on 5th day of inoculation from incubator, kill them by chilling and remove CAMs and embryos for pathological examination. Preserve the harvested material in deep freezer for future use.

Results

Note down the mortality pattern of embryos and pathological lesions including confluent and/or pock on CAMs and record in the table on the next page.

QUESTIONS

1. Name the family and the genus to which ILT virus belongs.

Embryo No.	Day of mortality of embryo, if any	Type of pathological lesions on CAM
1		
2		
3		
4		
5		

2. What is the difference between pathogenicity of ILT and IB diseases of poultry? When were these two diseases first reported from India?

EXERCISE 14

CULTIVATION OF FOWL POX VIRUS IN EMBRYONATED CHICKEN EGGS BY CHORIOALLANTOIC MEMBRANE ROUTE

Materials

Fowl pox infected skin feather follicles and comb with lesions from Exercise 1, 10-12 days old chicken embryos 5, egg incubator, drill machine, egg candler, syringes and needles, forceps, scissors, petridish, tincture of iodine, melted paraffin, phosphate buffer saline, penicillin and streptomycin.

Procedure

1. Take out the frozen fowl pox infected skin from deep freezer, thaw at room temperature. Triturate the tissue in mortar and pestle and prepare 10% suspension.
2. Centrifuge the suspension at 2500 RPM for 20 minutes and remove the supernatant in a sterile test tube.
3. Treat the fluid with penicillin and streptomycin at room temperature for 20 minutes and inoculate on media for sterility test.
4. Inoculate 0.1 ml in each egg by CAM route and incubate the eggs at 37°C in egg incubator.
5. Examine the eggs each day by candling and change the sides of the eggs. Discard the eggs dying within 24 hours of inoculation.
6. On 5th day remove all the eggs from incubator, kill the embryos by chilling and collect CAM. Wash the CAM in a petridish with normal saline solution and examine for pock or confluent lesions. Also examine lesions on the embryos.

Results

Note down the lesions on CAM and embryo in the table on the next page.

QUESTIONS

1. What type of pathological lesions are found in chickens due to fowl pox virus?

Embryo No.	Day of embryo death, if any	Type of lesions on CAM and embryos
1		
2		
3		
4		
5		

EXERCISE 15

CULTIVATION OF INFECTIOUS BURSAL DISEASE (IBD) VIRUS IN EMBRYONATED CHICKEN EGGS BY CHORIOALLANTOIC MEMBRANE ROUTE

Materials

Bursa of Fabricius of chickens infected with IBD (from Exercise 1), 10-12 days old embryonated chicken eggs 5, egg incubator, drill machine, egg candler, syringes and needles, forceps, scissors, petridish, tincture of iodine, melted paraffin.

Procedure

1. Thaw frozen bursa of Fabricius from IBD infected birds at room temperature and triturate in mortar and pestle to make 10% suspension.
2. Centrifuge the suspension at 2500 RPM for 20 minutes and collect supernatant in a sterile tube.
3. Treat the fluid with penicillin and streptomycin at room temperature for 20 minutes.
4. Inoculate 0.2 ml in each of the 5 eggs by CAM route and incubate the eggs in egg incubator.
5. Examine the eggs every day for any mortality and change the sides of the eggs. Remove any dead egg from the incubator.
6. Remove all the remaining eggs from incubator on 5th day. Most of the eggs are expected to die within 3-5 days.
7. Chill the eggs in refrigerator and remove CAMs and embryos.

Results

Examine embryos and CAMs for pathological lesions and record observations in the table on the next page.

QUESTIONS

1. Name the family and genus of IBD virus.

Embryo No.	Day of death of embryo	Pathological lesions on CAM and embryo
1		
2		
3		
4		
5		

2. Briefly describe the properties of IBD virus including that of its genome.
3. Describe the pathogenicity of IBD and how the disease affects the resistance of the chickens to other infectious diseases?
4. Name the vaccine(s), dose, route of vaccination and immunity offered by IBD vaccine(s).

EXERCISE 16

CULTIVATION OF AVIAN ENCEPHALOMYELITIS VIRUS IN EMBRYONATED CHICKEN EGGS BY YOLK SAC ROUTE

Materials

Brain tissue from chicken infected with encephalomyelitis virus (from Exercise 1), 7 day incubated eggs 5, egg incubator, drill machine, egg candler, syringes and needles, forceps, scissors, petridish, pipette, tincture of iodine, melted paraffin, phosphate buffer saline, penicillin and streptomycin, centrifuge machine.

Procedure

1. Take out the brain tissue of chicken infected with encephalomyelitis from deep freezer and thaw it at room temperature.
2. Macerate the brain in test tube with the help of a pipette and make 10% emulsion by adding phosphate buffer saline.
3. Centrifuge the suspension at 2500 RPM for 20 minutes and remove supernatant in another sterilized tube.
4. Treat the suspension with penicillin and streptomycin at room temperature for 20 minutes. Test the fluid for sterility on blood agar plates and in thioglycollate broth.
5. Inoculate 5 eggs by yolk sac route, the amount being 0.25 ml per egg.
6. Incubate the eggs at 37°C in egg incubator and examine them daily by candling. Remove dead embryos, if any, and all the remaining embryos after 3 days incubation, chill them and collect yolk, yolk sac and brain of the embryos.
7. Preserve the material in screw-cap tube and freeze in deep freezer for future use.

Results

Record the observations in the table on the next page.

QUESTIONS

1. Name the family and genus of avian encephalomyelitis virus.

Egg No.	Day of death of embryo	Pathological changes in embryo, yolk and yolk sac
1		
2		
3		
4		
5		

2. Describe important properties of avian encephalomyelitis virus including its size, symmetry of capsid, No. of capsomeres, if any, and nature of genome.
3. Avian encephalomyelitis virus is an enterovirus. How does it affect the brain of chickens causing encephalomyelitis rather than causing gastroenteritis? Has this disease been reported from India?

C. Cultivation of Viruses in Cell Cultures

Cultures prepared with dispersed cells are designated as cell cultures. Tissue cultures on the other hand are those cell systems which are established with tissue fragments or masses of cells originating from the fragments. Several techniques such as slide cultures in which tissue fragments are embedded in plasma clots on glass surfaces, flask cultures in which cells are grown in suspension, and cell cultures as monolayers on glass surfaces, are employed for cultivating cells in an artificial media. The advantages of cultivating viruses in cell culture systems are :

1. They are free from antibodies, hormones and similar other host factors.
2. Different viruses produce specific metabolic and cytopathic changes.
3. Cell lines from different species and organs are available. Primary cell cultures can be prepared from different species or organs as per the needs of specific viruses.

Most commonly used tissues for cell culture preparations are kidneys and testes from young animals like lambs, kids, calves and piglets. Chicken embryo kidneys and fibroblast cell cultures are also commonly used.

The preparation of tissues for cell culture involves collection of fresh tissues in balanced salt solution (BSS), cutting the tissue in small pieces with scissors, and then washing with BSS. The minced tissue cells are treated with trypsin in special flask with magnetic stirrer to prepare cultures with a uniform layer of cells. The cells are washed 2-3 times to free them from trypsin. Most of the cell culture work is done with fluid medium in stationary tubes, flasks or petridishes. Flat sided prescription and milk dilution bottles are also frequently used. The tubes and flasks with cells and growth medium are tightly closed before incubation. The humidity in the incubator should be about 85% and CO_2 5-8%. The cells will grow and form a sheet on the walls of the tube or flask. The medium has to be replaced in between due to development of acidity by the metabolizing cells. When cell sheet is formed, it is inoculated with virus and growth medium is replaced with maintenance medium which has minimum serum. The virus will multiply in the cells and may show cytopathic and other changes.

Cell culture monolayers are widely used for isolation of viruses from clinical samples. Tissues from embryos grow more rapidly than the tissues from young animals. Tissues from adult animals are difficult to grow. Three different kinds of cell cultures are :

1. **Primary cell cultures :** They are initiated usually from tissues of animals or chicken embryos. They are very satisfactory for virus cultivation and consist of both epithelial and fibroblastic cells.
2. **Diploid cell strains :** They are serially propagated primary cell cultures and retain a normal set of chromosomes. These primary cell cultures can be serially transferred few times but generally not more than 5 or 6 times.
3. **Permanent cell lines :** These are cells with an abnormal chromosome number (heteroploidy) and morphology that are capable of maintaining indefinitely in vitro by serial transfer. Examples of permanent cell lines are Hela, PK_{15} (pig kidney), Vero (African Gr. monkey kidney), BHK_{21} (baby hamster kidney) etc.

In the next few exercises kidney cell cultures from chicken embryos, young chicks and lambs will be prepared or demonstrated. For the preparation of tissue culture media, various reagents and buffers are used (see Appendix A).

EXERCISE 17

PREPARATION OF CHICKEN EMBRYO KIDNEY CELL CULTURES

Materials

Embryonated chicken eggs 16-18 days old 5, Hanks' balanced salt solution (BSS), growth medium, 0.25% trypsin in Hanks' BSS, sterile beakers (different sizes) covered with aluminium foil, sterile forceps, scalpels, and scissors (straight and curved), two sterile 500 ml Erlenmeyer trypsinization flasks, one inch teflon coated magnetic bars and stirrer, sterile 3 × 3 inch gauze pads, sterile 50 ml graduated conical centrifuge tubes, 60 × 15 mm petridish, Leighton tube, 16 × 150 mm sterile culture tubes in a rack covered with aluminium foil, No. 0 sterile silicone stoppers in a beaker (autoclaved).

Procedure

1. Disinfect egg shell over air sac, break the shell and remove it leaving about 5-6 mm above air sac base.
2. Remove shell membrane and CAM with a forceps, pick up the neck of the embryo and lift it up, cut the yolk sac from the body and place the embryo in a sterile petridish.
3. Cut the neck and legs with scissors and discard them.
4. Pick up the skin with forceps and make a transverse cut of skin with scissors and cut the body posterior to the ribs. Hold up the posterior portion of the body and cut the viscera with curved scissors and discard.
5. With the help of curved forceps, remove kidneys from 5 embryos and place them in a petridish containing about 20 ml BSS. (Cell cultures from kidney, from young or adult chickens can also be processed in this manner.)
6. Rinse the kidneys several times with BSS and cut them into 1-2 mm pieces with the help of a scalpel. Wash the kidney pieces 3-4 times with BSS, and discard BSS.
7. With the help of forceps, remove kidney fragments and transfer them in an Erlenmeyer flask containing a teflon covered stirring bar and 0.25% trypsin in BSS with a pH of 8.0-8.4. Add about 50 ml trypsin solution.
8. Place the flask on the magnetic stirrer and carry out trypsinization at room temperature (25°C) for about 1 hour. After this, pour cell suspension through 2 layers of cheese

cloth. (If necessary the remaining tissue can be retrypsinized by adding fresh trypsin, cells separated through cheese cloth and added in the cell filtrate collected earlier.)

9. The filtered cell suspension is taken in a conical graduated centrifuge tubes of 50 ml size and centrifuged in a refrigerated centrifuge for 5 minutes at 1500 RPM. Discard supernatant fluid, add an equal amount of fresh BSS in the tube, mix the content and repeat washing twice to free the cells of trypsin.
10. Estimate the volume of packed cells and add required amount of growth medium to obtain desired concentration of cells in growth medium. Normally a 10^{-2} dilution of 1 ml packed chicken embryo kidney cells contain approximately 1×10^7 cells. For more accurate estimation of cells counting can be done in a haemocytometer. For monolayers add 4 ml of 1×10^7 cells/ml in 60 × 15 mm petridish, and 1 ml of 2×10^6 cells/ml in a 16 × 150 mm culture tube or in a Leighton tube (with cover slip).
11. Incubate the cultures properly stoppered at 37°C under 6-8% CO_2 and 80% humidity. The monolayer of cells is expected to be ready by next day. The culture tubes are incubated at an angle of about 5°.
12. Examine the monolayer cell sheet in petridish and tubes by inverted tissue culture microscope and cell culture sheet on cover slip (from Leighton tube) after fixing in 10% neutral formalin and staining with haematoxylin and eosin under compound light microscope.

Results

Examine cell culture(s) and draw diagram of cell sheet, indicating magnification.

Cell sheet in petridish
Magnification ....

Cell sheet on coverslip
Magnification ....

EXERCISE 18

PREPARATION OF LAMB KIDNEY CELL CULTURES

Materials

Lamb kidney, Hanks' balanced salt solution, 0.25% trypsin (1 : 250), lactalbumin hydrolysate growth medium, culture tube (16 × 150 mm), scissors, scalpels, forceps, pipettes, Erlenmeyer flask, magnetic stirrer, centrifuge tubes, beakers and other equipments for cell culture.

Procedure

1. Kill the lamb after anaesthetizing with pentobarbital solution, clip hair from abdomen, swab abdomen with 70% alcohol and then with tincture of iodine.
2. A midline incision is made posterior to the sternum. The abdominal wall is reflected sideways thereby exposing the abdominal viscera.
3. Remove kidneys aseptically and put in a sterile beaker covered with aluminium foil. The beaker should contain sufficient Hanks' BSS to cover the kidneys.
4. Transfer the kidneys to a sterile petridish, peel off the capsule and cut the kidneys in half longitudinally. Cut the cortex portion with curved scissors, and mince finely. Discard medulla from both kidneys. (Kidney cell cultures from calf, kid and piglets can also be prepared by following the technique described in this exercise.)
5. Transfer the minced tissue in a 500 ml trypsinizing flask and wash thrice with Hanks' BSS.
6. Add trypsin solution to the minced tissue at the rate of about 40-50 ml per gm of tissue. Drop teflon stirring bar in the flask and place it on a magnetic stirrer and allow to stir for about 1 hour at room temperature.
7. After trypsinization, filter cell suspension through 3 layers of cheese cloth and pour cell suspension in a conical graduated centrifuge tube of 50 ml capacity.
8. Centrifuge the suspension in a refrigerated centrifuge for 10 minutes at 1500 RPM. Decant the supernatant fluid, add equal amount of fresh BSS to the tube, mix the content and repeat washing twice. Pool the suspension in one tube if it is in more than one tube.
9. Add 0.5 ml cell suspension (0.5×10^{-2} dilution of packed cells in LAH growth medium) in each 16 × 150 mm culture tube and incubate at 37°C for 3-5 days.

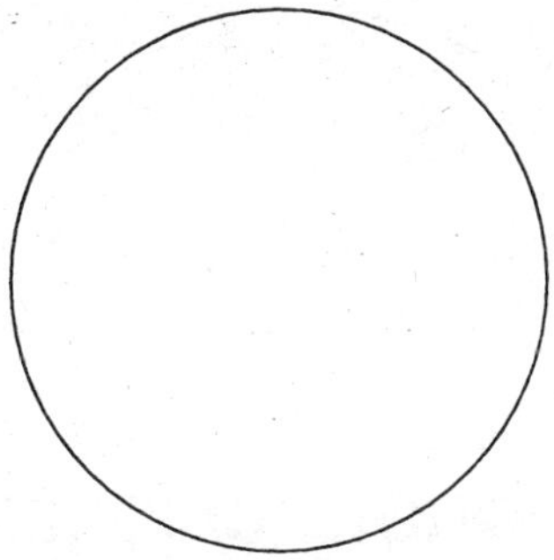

Cell sheet in culture tube
Magnification ……

10. Examine the monolayer cell sheet under inverted tissue culture microscope and preserve for future use after replacing growth medium with maintenance medium.

Results

Note down the time when attachment of cells is complete on glass and the time when monolayer cell sheet is complete. Make drawing of cell sheet in culture tube.

QUESTIONS

1. What will happen if cell suspension is not thoroughly washed of trypsin before adding LAH growth medium and incubation?
2. What is the difference between LAH growth medium and LAH maintenance medium?
3. Give details of cell counting by haemocytometer.

EXERCISE 19

PREPARATION OF WHOLE CHICKEN EMBRYO CELL CULTURES

Materials

Embryonated chicken eggs 9-10 days old, Hanks' BSS, 0.25% trypsin (1 : 250) in BSS, lactalbumin hydrolysate growth medium, 60 × 15 mm petridish, 16 × 150 mm culture tube, scalpels, scissors, pipettes, forceps, Erlenmeyer flask, magnetic stirrer, containers for cells and other equipments for cell culture work.

Procedure

1. Sterilize egg shell over air sac with tincture of iodine, crack shell over air sac with forceps and remove it leaving at the base about 5 mm.
2. Break the shell membrane and CAM from air sac opening, take out the embryo by holding its neck with forceps, cut yolk sac with scissors and place the embryo in a petridish containing about 20 ml BSS.
3. Wash the embryo in BSS and transfer it in another petridish. Cut head, feet, wings and viscera and discard them.
4. Cut the embryo in small pieces (3-4 mm size) with scalpel and add slightly warmed 15-20 ml BSS, wash the tissue thoroughly and discard the BSS. Repeat washing thrice.
5. Transfer the fragments in an Erlenmeyer flask containing teflon-covered stirring bar and 0.25% trypsin in BSS of pH 8.2. The amount of trypsin solution for each embryo will be about 40 ml. Now place the flask on the magnetic stirrer and carry out trypsinization for 1 hour at room temperature.
6. Filter the cells through 2-layer cheese cloth and transfer in a 50 ml conical graduated centrifuge tube and spin at 1500 RPM for 5 min. in a refrigerated centrifuge. Discard the supernatant, add equal amount of fresh BSS in the tube, mix the contents and repeat washing twice.
7. Estimate the volume of packed cells and add required amount of LAH culture medium to obtain desired concentration of cells/ml. (It is estimated that 10^{-2} dilution of packed chicken embryo cells will contain about 1×10^{7} cells per ml.)
8. Add 4 ml in a 60 × 15 mm petridish, and 1 ml in a 16 × 150 mm culture tube or Leighton

tube and incubate at 37°C in an atmosphere of 80-85% humidity. The tubes are incubated at an angle of about 5°.

9. The cell sheet will be ready by 2nd or 3rd day when the growth medium will be replaced by maintenance medium and cell culture tubes/plates are preserved.

Results

Note down the observations including the time of cell attachment to the glass and time when complete sheet is formed. Make drawing of cell sheets in culture tube and petridish.

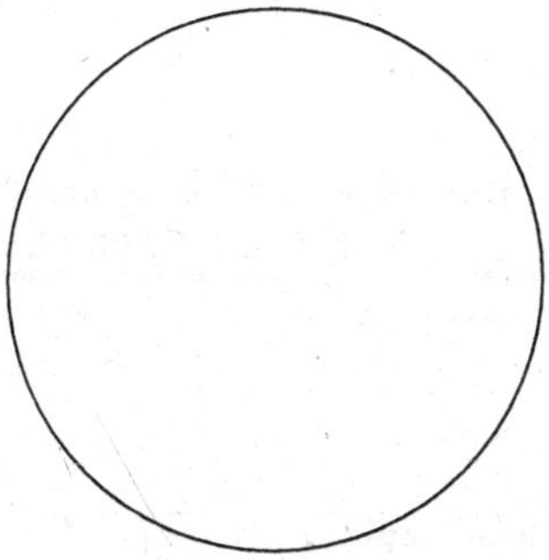

Cell sheet in petridish
Magnification ....

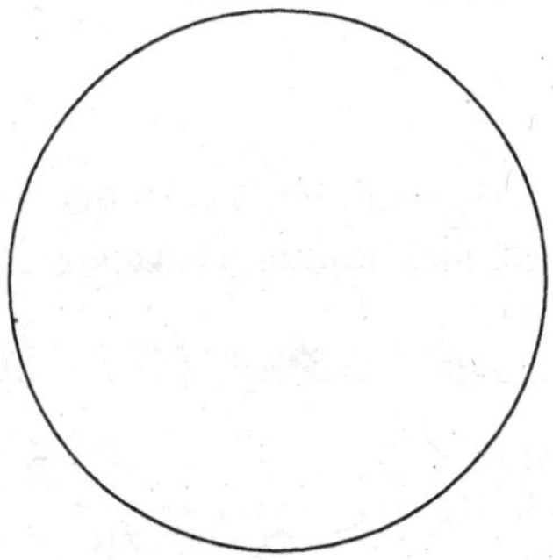

Cell sheet in culture tube
Magnification ....

QUESTIONS

1. Name the type of cells in a whole chicken embryo monolayer cell culture and the virus(es) which can be cultivated in such cell cultures.

EXERCISE 20

MAINTENANCE AND TRANSFER OF CELL CULTURES

Materials

LAH growth medium, LAH maintenance medium, Hanks' BSS, versene-trypsin solution, centrifuge tubes, culture tubes and bottles and other equipments for cell culture work.

1. MAINTAINING PRIMARY CELL CULTURES

Procedure

1. Remove LAH growth medium from monolayer cell sheet.
2. Add adequate amount of LAH maintenance medium in the cell culture tube or flask. The maintenance medium either contains no serum or contains only 2% serum. Maintain the culture at 4°C.
3. Change maintenance medium every 4-6 days when it becomes acidic.

By following the above procedure, primary cell cultures can be maintained for a short period. To maintain the cells for a longer periods, they have to be subcultured in growth medium.

2. TRANSFER OR SUBCULTURE OF PRIMARY CELLS

Normally mammalian cells can be serially transferred up to 5 or 6 passages. Some cells can be serially transferred many passages.

Procedure

1. Remove maintenance medium from the monolayer cell culture and wash it with Hanks' BSS for several seconds.
2. Add versene-trypsin solution equal to the original volume of the maintenance medium and incubate at 37°C until cells detach from the glass. In between, the tube/bottle should be shaken. Generally cells will be detached within 5-10 min.
3. Centrifuge the cells for about 5 min. at 1500 RPM in a refrigerated centrifuge. Pour off the supernatant fluid and transfer and resuspend the cells in required amount of growth medium. Make sure that clumps of cells are broken and cell concentration is maintained as mentioned in preceding exercises.
4. The suspension is now ready for seeding in tubes or bottles.

EXERCISE 21

PRESERVATION OF CELL CULTURES IN DEEP FREEZER OR IN LIQUID NITROGEN

Cells which are not needed very frequently can be preserved by freezing for a long time. By doing so there is no need for repeated transfer or subculture. Cells can be preserved by storing at –70°C in deep freezer or in liquid nitrogen (–196°C). For successful preservation, the cells should be frozen slowly and cell suspension should contain 5-10% dimethyl sulfoxide. The freezing medium should also have higher concentration of serum. The recovery of the cells should be by rapid thawing.

Materials

Cell culture, freezing medium, growth medium, ampoules, pipettes, mechanical freezer, water bath, dimethyl sulfoxide, arrangement for sealing ampoules, container with liquid N_2, bottles and tubes.

Procedure

1. Suspend cells in freezing medium (growth medium with twice the normal amount of serum) with higher concentration of cells. The cell count may be $2–5 \times 10^6$ per ml.
2. Add 5-10% dimethyl sulfoxide in cell suspension mixing thoroughly.
3. Add 1 ml cell suspension in each neutral glass ampoule, seal and label.
4. Freeze the ampoules slowly either by mechanical means or by slowly lowering the temperature of dry ice-alcohol bath manually.
5. Maintain the ampoules in liquid nitrogen as long as desired.
6. For recovery, remove the ampoule and rapidly thaw in a water bath maintained at 40°C. The ampoule should also be agitated in between.
7. Suspend the cells of one ampoule in 12 ml growth medium and culture in bottles, tubes or flasks.

Results

Compare the percentage of recovery of cells preserved in deep freezer and liquid nitrogen.

EXERCISE 22

CULTIVATION OF RANIKHET DISEASE VIRUS IN WHOLE CHICKEN EMBRYO MONOLAYER CELL CULTURES

This exercise will also serve the purpose of observing the cytopathic effect (CPE) and determination of the titre of the virus.

Materials

Ranikhet disease virus (allantoic fluid from Exercise 12), whole chicken embryo cell culture tubes (from Exercise 19), LAH maintenance medium, Hanks' BSS (without phenol red), diluent, tubes, pipettes and other equipments for cell culture work.

Procedure

Preparation of virus dilutions

1. Arrange 10 tubes in a rack and label them serially 1 to 10.
2. Add 0.9 ml diluent in each tube.
3. Add 0.1 ml Ranikhet disease virus in tube No. 1 and prepare 10-fold serial dilutions of the virus as shown in the table below :

Tubes	1	2	3	4	5	6	7	8	9	10
Diluent (ml)	0.9	0.9	0.9	0.9	0.9	0.9	0.9	0.9	0.9	0.9
	+	+	+	+	+	+	+	+	+	+
Virus	0.1 →	0.1 →	0.1 →	0.1 →	0.1 →	0.1 →	0.1 →	0.1 →	0.1 →	0.1
	Mix diluent and virus in tube No. 1 and transfer 0.1 ml to tube No. 2. Mix the contents of tube No. 2 and transfer 0.1 ml to tube No. 3. Continue mixing and transfer of virus-diluent mixture up to tube No. 10.									
Final virus dilution	10^{-1}	10^{-2}	10^{-3}	10^{-4}	10^{-5}	10^{-6}	10^{-7}	10^{-8}	10^{-9}	10^{-10}

Inoculation of cell culture tubes with virus to find out the titre and observe CPE

1. Arrange 10 chicken embryo monolayer cell culture tubes in another rack and label them serially 1 to 10.

2. Pour off the medium from all cell culture tubes and add 0.25 ml of different virus dilutions prepared above in such a manner that tube No. 1 gets 10^{-1} dilution, tube No. 2, 10^{-2} dilution and so on till the last tube i.e. tube No. 10 gets 10^{-10} virus dilution.
3. Spread the virus inoculum uniformly on the entire monolayer cell sheet in all tubes and incubate them at 37°C for virus adsorption.
4. Remove the tubes from incubator after 1 hour and pour off the excess of virus inoculum, wash the culture tubes with Hanks' BSS twice and add 1 ml of maintenance medium in each tube and incubate at 37°C at an angle of 5°.
5. Examine the culture tubes daily for 3 to 4 days and record CPE in the table.

Results

Culture tubes with virus dilution	Cytopathic effects*
10^{-1}	
10^{-2}	
10^{-3}	
10^{-4}	
10^{-5}	
10^{-6}	
10^{-7}	
10^{-8}	
10^{-9}	
10^{-10}	

* Score per tube : +++ = Maximum CPE, ++ = Medium CPE, + = Minimum CPE, 0 = No CPE

Virus titre showing CPE in highest dilution =

QUESTIONS

1. Briefly describe the type of CPE produced in bovine monolayer cell cultures by :
   (a) Sheep pox virus
   (b) Parainfluenza virus
   (c) Infectious bovine rhinotracheitis virus
   (d) Rinderpest virus
   (e) Foot and mouth disease virus
   (f) Bovine enteroviruses
2. Name primary cell cultures which will support the growth of the following viruses. Also mention the type of CPE produced by them.
   (a) Hog cholera
   (b) Equine rhinopneumonitis
   (c) Equine encephalomyelitis
   (d) Canine distemper
   (e) Canine hepatitis
   (f) Fowl pox

EXERCISE 23

CULTIVATION AND TITRATION OF RANIKHET DISEASE VIRUS IN WHOLE CHICKEN EMBRYO CELL CULTURES BY AGAR OVERLAY PLAQUE COUNTING METHOD

Enumerative response is one of the methods of virus titration. In this method the viral infectivity is measured by focal lesions like plaque counting in monolayer cell cultures, pock counting on CAMs of embryonated eggs etc.

Materials

Ranikhet disease virus (allantoic fluid from Exercise 12), whole chicken embryo monolayer cell culture plates 60 × 15 mm (from Exercise 19), agar overlay medium tubes (4 ml in each tube), Hanks' BSS (without phenol red), tubes, pipettes, and other equipments for cell culture work.

Procedure

1. Serially prepare 10-fold virus dilutions from 10^{-1} to 10^{-10} in test tubes. For this follow instructions given in Exercise 22.
2. For virus inoculation, arrange 10 monolayer cell culture plates and label them serially 1 to 10.
3. Pour off the medium from cell culture plates and wash them individually with 3 to 4 ml BSS.
4. Inoculate cell culture plates with 0.5 ml of the respective virus dilutions in such a way that plate No. 1 is inoculated with 10^{-1} virus dilution, plate No. 2 with 10^{-2} virus dilution. The plate inoculation will continue serially till the last plate i.e. plate No. 10 which is inoculated with 10^{-10} virus dilution.
5. Spread the virus inoculum uniformly on the entire cell sheet of each plate and incubate the plates at 37°C for 1 hour.
6. After virus adsorption, take out the plates from incubator and wash them twice with BSS. Discard the washings, add 4 ml of agar overlay medium to each plate and allow the agar to set. Return all the plates to incubator.
7. Examine the culture plates under low power microscope on 3rd or 4th day for plaque

formation. To stain the culture plates, add 0.5 ml neutral red stain to each plate, spread the stain uniformly and incubate the plates for 30 minutes at 37°C and for 1 hour at 4°C.

8. Count the plaques by a colony counter and calculate the titre of the virus as plaque forming units (pfu) per ml in undiluted allantoic fluid.

Results

Record the result in the following table and draw a diagram showing distribution of plaques in the culture plates.

Cell culture plates	1	2	3	4	5	6	7	8	9	10
Virus dilution	10^{-1}	10^{-2}	10^{-3}	10^{-4}	10^{-5}	10^{-6}	10^{-7}	10^{-8}	10^{-9}	10^{-10}
No. of plaques in 0.5 ml										

Calculations

No. of plaques in 0.5 ml =

No. of plaques in 1 ml undiluted allantoic fluid =

QUESTIONS

1. What are different methods of virus titration?

Serology

Similar to bacterial antibodies, viral antibodies are produced in the blood sera of human beings and animals due to viral infections. The viral antibodies in sera are detected by various viral antigen and antibody reactions. The most commonly used antigen antibody reactions are :

1. Precipitation
2. Complement fixation
3. Fluorescent antibody technique
4. Enzyme linked immunosorbent assay (ELISA)
5. Haemagglutination inhibition (HI)
6. Virus neutralization (VN)

The HI and VN tests are applicable only in viral antigen antibody reactions. All other tests are applied both to bacterial and viral serological reactions.

The students are advised to refer to "Laboratory Manual of Veterinary Microbiology, Part II, Immunology and Serology" by the author for other details pertaining to this section. In the following few exercises laboratory tests for HA, HI and VN will be described.

EXERCISE 24

TITRATION OF RANIKHET DISEASE VIRUS BY HAEMAGGLUTINATION TEST

This is not an antigen-antibody test. The titre of haemagglutination of the virus is found out before carrying out the haemagglutination inhibition test.

Materials

Ranikhet disease virus (allantoic fluid from Exercise 12), 0.5% chicken RBCs suspension, normal saline solution and other equipments for conducting the test including pipettes, tubes, and microtitre plate.

Procedure

Preparation of virus dilutions

1. Arrange 10 tubes (12 × 100 mm) in a rack and label them serially 1 to 10.
2. Prepare two-fold serial dilutions of the virus in normal saline beginning with 1 : 2 dilution in tube No. 1 through 1 : 1024 dilution in tube No. 10 as shown in the following table.

Tubes	1	2	3	4	5	6	7	8	9	10
Normal saline	0.5	0.5	0.5	0.5	0.5	0.5	0.5	0.5	0.5	0.5
	+	+	+	+	+	+	+	+	+	+
Virus (undiluted)	0.5 →	0.5 →	0.5 →	0.5 →	0.5 →	0.5 →	0.5 →	0.5 →	0.5 →	0.5
	Mix normal saline and virus in tube No. 1 and transfer 0.5 ml to tube No. 2. Mix the contents of tube No. 2 and transfer 0.5 ml to tube No. 3. Continue such mixing and transfer of virus-saline mixture up to tube No. 10 to make two-fold serial dilutions.									
Final virus dilution	1/2	1/4	1/8	1/16	1/32	1/64	1/128	1/256	1/512	1/1024

All above figures are in ml.

Haemagglutination test

1. In a microtitre plate label 11 wells in a row from 1 to 11. Well No. 11 will act as RBCs control.
2. Add virus dilutions from 1 : 2 to 1 : 1024 in well No. 1 to 10; the quantity of virus dilutions in each well will be 0.25 ml.

3. Now add 0.25 ml RBCs suspension (0.5%) in all the wells including well No. 11. The details of HA test in tabular form are shown below :

Wells in microtitre tray	1	2	3	4	5	6	7	8	9	10	11 RBC control
Virus dilutions	0.25	0.25	0.25	0.25	0.25	0.25	0.25	0.25	0.25	0.25	0.0
	The virus dilution will be 1 : 2 in 1st well, 1 : 4 in 2nd well. The virus dilutions will be added serially until well No. 10 which will have 1 : 1024 virus dilution.										
RBCs suspension	0.25	0.25	0.25	0.25	0.25	0.25	0.25	0.25	0.25	0.25	0.25

All figures are in ml.

4. Shake the plate well to mix the reagents and incubate at room temperature for haemagglutination. Examine the plate every 15 minutes up to 1 hour for uniform agglutination covering the bottom of wells of plate.

Interpretation

A positive HA test consists of a layer of uniformly agglutinated cells covering the bottom of the wells of the plate. Such a pattern is designated by plus (+) sign. A negative test consists of a compact disk of sedimented cells in the centre of the bottom of well of the plate similar to control. This is designated by minus (–) sign.

Results

Record the end point of HA activity of the virus in the following table. The end point of HA is the highest dilution of the virus showing agglutination.

Wells in perspex tray	1	2	3	4	5	6	7	8	9	10
Virus dilution	1/2	1/4	1/8	1/16	1/32	1/64	1/128	1/256	1/512	1/1024
End point of HA*										

* Score : + = positive reaction, – = negative reaction

HA titre in 1 ml undiluted virus =

QUESTIONS

1. Differentiate between haemagglutination and haemadsorption.
2. Name various haemagglutinating viruses.
3. Discuss the nature of haemagglutinins. Are they antigens or enzymes?

EXERCISE 25

HAEMAGGLUTINATION INHIBITION (HI) TEST WITH RANIKHET DISEASE VIRUS-SERUM MIXTURE

In this test alpha procedure, i.e., decreasing virus-constant serum will be followed.

Materials

Ranikhet disease virus dilutions 1/2 to 1/2048 (two-fold dilutions) as prepared in Exercise 24, antiserum from fowls vaccinated with RD virus strain R_2B (undiluted), normal saline solution, 0.5% fowl RBCs suspension, microtitre plate on a stand with a mirror underneath, pipettes and other equipments for HI test.

Procedure

1. Serially number 1 to 12 wells of the microtitre plate in a row.
2. Add 0.25 ml of two-fold serial dilutions of the virus from 1 : 2 to 1 : 2048 in wells No. 1 to 11. Well No. 12 will act as RBCs control.
3. Next add 0.25 ml Ranikhet disease antiserum diluted to 1 : 5 in wells No. 1 to 11.
4. Mix the virus-serum reactants thoroughly and allow to act for 20 minutes at room temperature.
5. Now add 0.25 ml of 0.5% fowl RBCs suspension in all the 12 wells of the tray, mix the contents and allow to act for 45 minutes at room temperature before taking the reading.

Interpretation

The end point of the haemagglutination inhibition activity of the serum is the lowest dilution of the virus in which HA activity is completely inhibited.

For HA titre, the test of Ranikhet disease virus conducted in Exercise 24 should be taken into account for HI calculation.

Results

Calculation of the HI titre of the serum is done by the following formula :

$$\frac{\text{Virus end point (reciprocal)}}{\text{Serum end point (reciprocal)}} \times \text{Dilution of serum} = \text{HI titre}$$

HI titre in 1 ml undiluted serum =

EXERCISE 26

DETERMINATION OF HAEMAGGLUTINATION INHIBITION TITRES OF BIRDS VACCINATED WITH RANIKHET DISEASE VIRUS

In this exercise the students will practise calculation of HI titres of Ranikhet disease antisera 1, 2, 3 and 4.

Materials

Same as given in Exercise 25, and antisera 1, 2, 3 and 4. For the purpose of calculation of HI titres of different antisera, the HA titre of the virus may be considered as 512.

Procedure

As described in Exercise 25.

Results

The HA titre of Ranikhet disease virus and imaginary end points of HI activity of different antisera is tabulated below :

Cups in perspex tray	1	2	3	4	5	6	7	8	9	10
Virus dilutions	1/2	1/4	1/8	1/16	1/32	1/64	1/128	1/256	1/512	1/1024
Virus HA titre	+	+	+	+	+	+	+	+	+	–
Serum 1 (diluted 1 : 2) HI	+	+	–	–	–	–	–	–	–	–
Serum 2 (diluted 1 : 5) HI	+	+	+	+	+	+	+	+	–	–
Serum 3 (diluted 1 : 4) HI	+	+	+	–	–	–	–	–	–	–
Serum 4 (diluted 1 : 8) HI	+	+	+	+	+	–	–	–	–	–

+ = Haemagglutination, – = No haemagglutination

For the guidance of the students, the HI titre of antiserum 1 is calculated below :

Virus titre = 512

Virus dilution in which HA activity was inhibited by the serum = $\frac{1}{8}$

Dilution of the serum before use = 1 : 2

Calculation of HI titre = $\frac{512}{8} \times 2 = 128$

By following the above example calculate HI titres of :

1. Serum 2

2. Serum 3

3. Serum 4

QUESTIONS

1. Differentiate alpha and beta procedures of HI test.

EXERCISE 27

DETERMINATION OF LETHAL DOSE50 (LD50) OF RANIKHET DISEASE VIRUS IN EMBRYONATED CHICKEN EGGS

Another method of virus titration is by quantal dose-response. This method is employed with end point method of titration in which groups of animals, egg embryos or cell cultures are inoculated with certain dilutions of virus.

Materials

Ranikhet disease virus (virulent), embryonated chicken eggs, test tubes, pipettes, syringes and needles and normal saline.

Procedure

1. Arrange 11 test tubes in a rack and number them 1 to 11.
2. Prepare 10-fold serial dilutions of the virus in normal saline starting from 10^{-1} to 10^{-10}.
3. Starting from the highest serial dilution of the virus, inoculate a batch of 5 chicken embryos with each virus dilution via allantoic cavity route. The dose of virus in each embryo will be 0.1 ml.
4. Incubate the embryos in egg incubator for a period of 3 days. Examine the eggs every day for any death. Preserve dead eggs in refrigerator.
5. At the end of incubation period, examine the dead and survived embryos inoculated with each virus dilution and calculate LD_{50} by Reed and Muench formula.

For the purpose of calculation of LD_{50} dose of the virus, use the imaginary figures shown in the table below.

Tubes	1	2	3	4	5	6	7	8	9	10	11
Dilution of virus	10^{0}	10^{-1}	10^{-2}	10^{-3}	10^{-4}	10^{-5}	10^{-6}	10^{-7}	10^{-8}	10^{-9}	10^{-10}
Positive response*	5/5	5/5	5/5	5/5	5/5	5/5	5/5	5/5	3/5	0/5	0/5

* Denominator = No. of eggs inoculated; Numerator = No. of eggs died or survived

Calculations

It is clear from the above table that 3 out of 5 embryos died in 10^{-8} dilution. The titre of the virus in 10^{-8} dilution is 10^{8} (this is antilog of 10^{-8}). In this case the exact 50% end point will lie somewhere between 10^{-8} and 10^{-9} virus dilutions for which Reed and Muench formula will be applied.

Procedure for interpolation of 50% end point of viral activity :

Dilution of virus	10^{-7}	10^{-8}	10^{-9}
Mortality rate	5/5	3/5	0/5
Numbers died	5	3	0
Numbers survived	0	2	5
Accumulation total			
Died	8	3	0
Survived	0	2.	7
Mortality rate	8/8	3/5	0/7
% mortality	100	60 ↓ LD_{50}	0

The 50% end point can be determined by the following formula :

$$\frac{\text{\% mortality next above 50\%} - 50\%}{\text{\% mortality next above 50\%} - \text{\% mortality next below 50\%}} = \text{Proportionate distance}$$

$$\frac{60-50}{60-0} = 0.167 \text{ (say 0.2) proportionate distance}$$

Log lower dilution (dilution in which % mortality next above 50%) = –8.0

Proportionate distance (0.2) × log dilution factor (10) = –0.2

Sum (50% end point) = –8.2

Antilog of reciprocal of 50% end point = $10^{8.2}$ = 158,500,000 LD_{50}

Titre of LD_{50} per 0.1 ml = $10^{8.2}$ or 1.585×10^{8}

Titre of LD_{50} virus per 1 ml = $10^{9.2}$ or 1.585×10^{9}

QUESTIONS

1. Define log of a number.

EXERCISE 28

DETERMINATION OF LD_{50} OF RANIKHET DISEASE VIRUS AND ITS SERUM NEUTRALIZATION INDEX (LD_{50} NI) IN EMBRYONATED CHICKEN EGGS

Decreasing virus constant serum method will be used in this exercise. The data of the table from Exercise 27 will be used for calculation of LD_{50} of the virus.

Tubes	1	2	3	4	5	6	7	8	9	10
Dilution of the virus	10^{-1}	10^{-2}	10^{-3}	10^{-4}	10^{-5}	10^{-6}	10^{-7}	10^{-8}	10^{-9}	10^{-10}
Embryo death in virus dilution*	5/5	5/5	5/5	5/5	5/5	5/5	5/5	3/5	0/5	0/5
Embryo death in serum-virus mixture (imaginary)	5/5	5/5	5/5	5/5	4/5	1/5	0/5	0/5	0/5	0/5

* Denominator = number of eggs inoculated; Numerator = number of eggs died or survived

Calculations

It is indicated from the table that neutralizing antibody is present in the serum because the end point of viral activity in virus-serum mixture is lower than the virus alone. In the test 50% end point of virus-serum mixture is to be compared to the 50% end point of virus alone. The neutralizing index (NI) is the reciprocal of the difference between the two end points expressed in units of positive response like LD_{50} NI.

The 50% end point of the virus dilution is $10^{-8.2}$. For this calculation refer to Exercise 27.

The end point of virus-serum mixture is calculated as follows :

$$\frac{\%\text{ mortality next above }50\% - 50\%}{\%\text{ mortality next above }50\% - \%\text{ mortality next below }50\%} = \text{Proportionate distance}$$

$$\frac{83.3 - 50}{83.3 - 16.7} = \frac{33.3}{66.6} = 0.5 \text{ proportionate distance}$$

Log lower dilution (dilution in which % mortality next above 50%) = –5.0

Proportionate distance (0.2) × log dilution factor (10) = –0.5

Virus-serum mixture				
Dilution of virus	10^{-4}	10^{-5}	10^{-6}	10^{-7}
Mortality in serum-virus mixture	5/5	4/5	1/5	0/5
Numbers died	5	4	1	0
Numbers survived	0	1	4	5
Accumulation total				
Died	10	5	1	0
Survived	0	1	5	10
Mortality rate	10/10	5/6	1/6	0/10
% mortality	100	83.3	16.6	0

Sum 50% endpoint = –5.5

Reciprocal of LD_{50} dilution = $10^{5.5}$

The endpoint of the virus alone is LD_{50} log 8.2 (see Exercise 27)

The endpoint of virus-serum mixture is LD_{50} log 5.5

LD_{50} NI of serum = log 2.7 (8.2 – 5.5)

Neutralizing dose = 501.2 (say = 500, i.e., 5×10^2)

The students should be given additional exercises to practise calculation of LD_{50} doses of the viruses and their serum neutralization indices in embryonated chicken eggs.

EXERCISE 29

ISOLATION OF E. COLI BACTERIOPHAGE FROM SEWAGE

Bacteria are susceptible to infection with viruses called bacteriophages. Bacteriophages are present in situations where bacteria are present including intestinal tracts of man and animals, faeces, sewage etc. Like viruses, bacteriophages are intracellular parasites of bacteria. They are specific in their affinity for certain species of bacteria.

Materials

E. coli, sewage sample, nutrient broth, flask, tubes and serological pipettes.

Procedure

1. Centrifuge sewage suspension at 2500 RPM for 20 minutes and remove supernatant in another tube with the help of a pipette.
2. To a flask add 25 ml nutrient broth, add 1 ml of *E. coli* culture in log phase and 1 ml of supernatant fluid from sewage.
3. Incubate the flask overnight at 37°C.
4. Centrifuge a portion of the broth culture from the flask, remove the supernatant and filter the supernatant through a glass filter.
5. Add 10 ml nutrient broth in each of the two tubes and inoculate one tube with 0.1 ml of *E. coli* culture and 0.2 ml of the filtrate from bacterial culture from No. 4 above. Inoculate the 2nd tube of broth with 0.1 ml of *E. coli* culture to serve as control.
6. Incubate both tubes at 37°C and examine frequently for turbidity as an evidence of bacterial growth.
7. Presence of bacteriophage is indicated if there is no turbidity in the tube or turbidity appears and then disappears due to bacterial lysis. The control tube will show good turbidity.
8. The presence of bacteriophage may be tested by mixing serial dilutions of the phage and plating the phage dilution and *E. coli* culture on a nutrient agar plate. After overnight incubation the tiny plaques may be seen and counted on agar plate.

Results

Record the results obtained with tube cultures.

Tube containing filtrate :

Tube not containing filtrate :

References in Virology

1. Andrews, C., and Periera, H.G. *Viruses of Vertebrates*. 2nd edition. Bailliere, Tindall and Cox, London, 1967.
2. Betts, A.O., and York, C.J. *Viral and Rickettsial Infections of Animals*. Vol. 1. Academic Press, Inc., New York, N.Y., 1967.
3. Blair, J.E., Lennette, E.H., and Truant, J.P. (Eds.). *Manual of Clinical Microbiology*. American Society for Microbiology, Bethesda, Md., 1970.
4. Burnet, F.M. *Principles of Animal Virology*. 2nd edition. Academic Press Inc., New York, 1960.
5. Cunningham, C.H. *A Laboratory Guide in Virology*. 6th edition. Burgess Publishing Co., Minneapolis, Minn., 1966.
6. Habel, K., and Salzmann, N.P. *Fundamental Techniques in Virology*. Academic Press, New York, N.Y., 1969.
7. Hahon, N. (Ed.). *Selected Papers on Virology*. Prentice Hall, Inc., Englewood Cliffs, New Jersey, 1964.
8. Harris, R.J.C. (Ed.). *Techniques in Experimental Virology*. Academic Press Inc., New York, 1964.
9. Hsuing, G.D. *Diagnostic Virology*. Yale University Press, New Haven, Conn., 1964.
10. Kalter, S.S. *Procedures for Routine Laboratory Diagnosis of Virus and Rickettsial Diseases*. Burgess Publishing Co., Minneapolis, Minn., 1965.
11. Lennette, E.H., and Schmidt, N.J. *Diagnostic Procedures for Viral and Rickettsial Infections*. 4th edition. American Public Health Association, Inc., New York, N.Y., 1969.
12. Luria, S.E., Darnell Jr. J.E., Baltimore, D. and Campbell, A. *General Virology*, 3rd edition. Wiley, New York, 1978.
13. Mahanty, S.B. and Dutta, S.K. *Veterinary Virology*. Lea and Febiger, Philadelphia, 1981.
14. Maramorosch, K., and Koprowski, H. (Eds.). *Methods in Virology*, Vols. I, II, III, IV. Academic Press, New York, N.Y., 1967.
15. Mascoli, C.C. and Burrell, R.G. *Experimental Virology*. Burgess Publishing Co., Minneapolis, 1965.
16. Merchant, D.J., Kahn, R.H., and Murphy, W.H. *Handbook of Cell and Organ Culture*. 2nd edition. Burgess Publishing Co., Minneapolis, Minn., 1964.
17. Merchant, I.A., and Packer, R.A. *Veterinary Bacteriology and Virology*. 7th edition. Iowa State University Press, Ames, Iowa, 1967.

18. Methods for the Examination of Poultry Biologics. 2nd edition. National Academy of Sciences—National Research Council, Publication No. 1038, Washington, D.C., 1963.
19. Parker, R.L. *Methods of Tissue Culture*. 3rd edition. Paul B. Hoeber, Ind., New York, N.Y., 1961.
20. Pollard, M. (Ed.). *Perspectives in Virology*, Vol. I, II, III, IV. John Wiley and Sons, Inc., New York, 1959; Burgess Publishing Co., Minneapolis 1961; Harper & Rowe, Publishers, Inc., New York, 1963, 1965.
21. Rhodes, A.J., and Van Rooyen, C.E. *Textbook of Virology*. 4th edition. The Williams and Wilkins Co., Baltimore, 1962.
22. Roberts, A.W. and Carter, G.R. *Simplified and Economical Cell Culture Techniques for Laboratories Beginning Chemical Veterinary Virology*. Michigan State University, East Lansing Michigan, 1972.
23. Swain, R.H.A., and Dodds, T.C. *Clinical Virology*. E.S. Livingstone, Ltd., London, 1967.
24. Waterson, A.P. *Introduction to Animal Virology*. Cambridge University Press, London, 1961.

Appendix A

MEDIA AND REAGENTS FOR CELL CULTURES*

1. Hanks' balanced salt solution (BSS) (10 ×)

Solution A for 1 litre

$CaCl_2$	1.4 gm
H_2O (glass double distilled)	200.0 ml

Prepare in 1 litre Erlenmeyer flask. Sterilize in autoclave at 115°C for 10 min. Cool at room temperature.

Solution B for 1 litre

Glucose	10.0 gm
NaCl	80.0 gm
KCl	4.0 gm
$MgSO_4 \cdot 7H_2O$	2.0 gm
KH_2PO_4	0.6 gm
$Na_2HPO_4 \cdot 12H_2O$	1.2 gm
Phenol red (0.2%)	100.0 ml
H_2O (glass distilled)	800.0 ml

Prepare in 2 litre Erlenmeyer flask. Sterilize in autoclave at 115°C for 10 minutes. Cool at room temperature.

After the solutions are cooled, slowly add solution A to solution B with regular mixing. Dispense the mixture into screw-cap bottles, 100 ml in each and store at 4°C.

2. Sodium bicarbonate (1.4%)

$NaHCO_3$	3.5 gm
H_2O (glass distilled)	250.0 ml
Phenol red (0.2%)	2.5 ml

Dissolve $NaHCO_3$ in water and add in 20 ml quantity in 30 ml screw-cap vials. Sterilize in autoclave at 121°C for 15 min and keep at 4°C.

3. Trypsin (0.25%)

Difco trypsin (1 : 250) is generally used.

Trypsin (1 : 250)	0.5 gm

---

* *Source*. Cunningham, C.H. **A Laboratory Guide in Virology**, 6th edition. Burgess Publishing Co., Minneapolis, Minn., 1966.

Hanks' BSS (10 ×) with phenol red	20.0 ml
$NaHCO_3$ with phenol red q.s. (pH 8.0)	4.0 ml
H_2O (distilled)	176.0 ml

Dissolve trypsin in $NaHCO_3$ and H_2O in a 200 ml volumetric flask and bring the vol. with H_2O.

Sterilize by Seitz filtration. Dispense into convenient sized prescription bottles and store at 4°C. Trypsin solution is generally prepared fresh each week.

4. Phosphate-buffered saline solution (PBS), pH 7.5 (without Ca or Mg ions)

NaCl	8.00 gm
KCl	0.20 gm
Na_2PO_4	1.15 gm
KH_2PO_4	0.20 gm
H_2O (distilled)	1,000.00 ml

Sterilize in the autoclave at 121°C and store at 4°C.

5. Phosphate-buffered saline solution (PBS), pH 7.4

Solution A	
NaCl	8.00 gm
KCl	0.20 gm
Na_2PO_4	1.15 gm
NH_2PO_4	0.20 gm
H_2O (distilled)	800.00 ml
Solution B	
$CaCl_2$	0.10 gm
H_2O	100.00 ml
Solution C	
$MgCl_2 \cdot 6H_2O$	0.10 gm
H_2O (distilled)	100.00 ml

Prepare each solution in a separate container. Sterilize in autoclave at 121°C for 15 min. After cooling the solutions, slowly add solutions B and C to solution A and store at 4°C.

6. $NaHCO_3$ (10% saturated)

$NaHCO_3$	10.0 gm
H_2O (distilled)	100.0 ml

Prepare in a flask and sterilize by Seitz filter. Store 20 ml quantity in 30 ml screw-cap vials at 4°C.

7. Phenol red (0.2%), 100 × stock solution

In a dry 200 ml volumetric flask add 0.4 gm of phenol red and then about 22 ml N/20 NaOH. Dissolve phenol red and then add glass double distilled water to make it 200 ml. Adjust pH to 7.0 with NaOH and then add water to volume. The solution should be bright red. Sterilize the solution in autoclave at 115°C for 10 minutes and store at 4°C.

8. Lactalbumin hydrolysate (LAH) 10 ×

For one litre

Lactalbumin hydrolysate	50 gm
Hanks' BSS (10 ×)	100 ml
H_2O (glass distilled)	900 ml

Dissolve LAH by heating gently in a water bath. Sterilize by Seitz filtration with positive pressure. Store at 4°C. The LAH will be used as a component of growth and maintenance medium as described below and the pH of medium will be adjusted with $NaHCO_3$.

9. Lactalbumin hydrolysate cultural medium

For 1 litre

Lactalbumin hydrolysate (10 ×)	100.0 ml
Hanks' BSS (10 ×)	77.0 ml
Penicillin	100,000 units
Streptomycin	1.0 mg
Heat inactivated newborn calf serum	
For growth medium	100 ml
For maintenance medium	20 ml
$NaHCO_3$ (1.4%) q.s. for pH 7.2-7.5	
H_2O (glass distilled) q.s.	1000.0 ml

The medium may be stored at 4°C for a limited period. For frequent use of this medium, smaller volume may be prepared.

10. Agar overlay medium for plaque assay technique

This is prepared by adding equal volumes of 2 × medium and 1.8% Special Agar-Noble (Difco) as follows :

Agar	1.8 gm
Hanks' BSS (1 ×) without phenol red	98.0 ml
$NaHCO_3$ without phenol red (1.4%)	2.0 ml

Dissolve agar with above ingredients in free flowing steam of autoclave. Distribute 2 ml of melted agar in 13 × 100 mm tubes, plug and sterilize at 121°C for 15 minutes. Store the tubes at 4°C until used.

When needed, place the tubes of agar in autoclave to melt in free flowing steam. Place tubes in a water bath at 45°C. Slightly warm 2 × medium in a water bath. With a pipette, transfer 2 ml of the medium to each tube of agar, mix the contents well and pour the medium on the cell culture in the petridish.

Neutral red for agar overlay medium

Neutral red	0.1 gm
Phosphate-buffered saline solution pH 7.0	100 ml

Dissolve neutral red in saline solution, filter through paper and store at 4°C. When required for plaque technique, make a fresh supply.

COUNTING OF CELLS FOR CELL CULTURE BY HAEMOCYTOMETER

Add 1 ml of trypan blue solution (0.4% in Hanks' BSS) to 0.5 ml of 10^{-2} cell suspension and mix well. Fill both chambers of haemocytometer with a capillary pipette. Count the unstained cells in the four corner squares and one central square of both chambers of haemocytometer. The No. of cells per ml in the original suspension will be :

Total No. of cells in 10 squares × 1000 × 3

With this information the packed cells can be suspended to the desired concentration.

Appendix B

PREFERRED SPECIMENS AND HOST SYSTEMS FOR ISOLATION OF THE VIRUSES FROM VIRAL INFECTIONS IN ANIMALS

Viral diseases	Specimens	Host system
1. Fowl pox	Skin, feather follicles, comb lesions	Cultivation in chicken embryos on CAM
2. Infectious laryngo-tracheitis	Trachea and lungs	Cultivation in chicken embryos on CAM
3. Infectious bronchitis	Trachea and lungs	In chicken embryos by allantoic cavity route
4. Newcastle disease	Lung, spleen and kidney	Cultivation in chicken embryos by allantoic route
5. Avian encephalo-myelitis	Brain	Cultivation in day old chicks by intracerebral route
6. Marek's disease	Intact cells from buffy coat, spleen, tumour tissues, lymphoid cells	In chicken embryo by CAM route and chicken kidney cell culture
7. Avian leucosis	Plasma, serum, tumour tissues like liver, spleen, kidneys etc. or embryos from infected chicken	In chicken embryo fibroblast cell culture
8. Avian influenza	Nasal swabs, trachea, lung	In chicken embryos by allantoic route
9. Infectious bursal disease	Bursa of Fabricius	In embryonated eggs by CAM route
10. Infectious bovine rhinotracheitis	Nasal and vaginal swabs, trachea, lung, kidney, foetal liver and kidney	In calf kidney and testes cell culture
11. Rinderpest	Blood at the height of temp., faeces, intestinal lymph glands, spleen	In calf kidney cell culture, vero cell culture
12. Bovine virus diarrhoea	Nasal and faecal swabs, spleen, lymph nodes, intestine, buffy coat	In bovine and ovine kidney and testes cell culture
13. Bovine parainfluenza	Nasal swabs, lungs	In bovine kidney and testes cell culture
14. Foot and mouth disease	Lymph from tongue and buccal cavity vesicles, foot and tongue lesions	In suckling mice, guinea pig foot pad, BHK21 cell line and calf kidney cell culture
15. Cow pox	Lymph from teat vesicles	In calf kidney cell culture
16. Malignant catarrhal fever	Thyroid and buffy coats of leucocytes	In cell culture of suspected tissue

Contd.

Viral diseases	Specimens	Host system
17. Calf diarrhoea rotavirus	Faecal swabs, infected intestine and lymph glands	In calf kidney and testes cell culture
18. Bovine enterovirus infection	Nasal and faecal swabs	In cell culture of bovine origin
19. Equine rhino-pneumonitis (equine abortion)	Nasal swabs, vaginal swabs, lung, fetal lung and liver	In equine kidney cell culture and PK15 cell line
20. Equine influenza	Nasal swabs, lung	In chicken embryos by allantoic route
21. Equine encephalo-myelitis (all forms)	Brain	In PK15 cell line, chicken embryos, various routes in suckling mice I/C
22. Vesicular stomatitis	Saliva and vesicular fluid	In chicken embryo CAM and most cell system
23. Equine infectious anaemia	Whole blood, leucocytes, serum	In primary horse leucocytes cell culture
24. African horse sickness	Lymph nodes, spleen, lung	In vero cell line and monkey kidney cell line
25. Sheep pox	Scabs from skin lesions	In lamb kidney and testes cell culture
26. Blue tongue	Blood at height of temp., saliva, swabs from eyes and nasal discharges, faecal swabs, lung, spleen	In chicken embryos by yolk sac route, in bovine and ovine kidney and testes cell culture, BHK21, Hela cell lines
27. Contagious pustular dermatitis	Skin lesions and scabs	In lamb kidneys and testes cell culture
28. Hog cholera	Spleen, lymph nodes, blood, nasal and eye swabs	In pig kidney, spleen, testes, lymph node cell cultures and PK15 cell line
29. Pseudorabies	Brain, tonsil, lung and kidney	In pig kidney cell line, in rabbit by S/C route
30. Transmissible gastroenteritis	Intestine	In primary pig kidney cell culture
31. African swine fever	Blood, tissue fluid, internal organs, eye and nasal swabs	In yolk sac of chicken embryos, pig, bovine and chicken kidney cell culture
32. Rabies	Brain	In suckling mice, chicken embryos (egg adapted), many cell lines including BHK21
33. Canine distemper	Lung, urinary bladder, cerebellum	In chicken embryo fibroblast cell culture, primary and continuous dog and ferret kidney cell culture
34. Canine hepatitis	Liver, kidney and lung	In canine kidney cell culture
35. Canine parvovirus disease	Intestinal scrappings, lymph nodes, spleen, liver, faecal samples	In canine foetal kidney, testes, and lymph node primary cell culture

Name of Student .... **Date** ....

Supplementary Exercise No. ......

Title ....

Materials :

Procedure :

Results :

Name of Student .... **Date** ....

Supplementary Exercise No. ......

Title ....

Materials :

Procedure :

Results :

Name of Student .... **Date** ....

Supplementary Exercise No. ......

Title ....

Materials :

Procedure :

Results :

Name of Student .... **Date** ....

Supplementary Exercise No. ......

Title ....

Materials :

Procedure :

Results :